ERIC FLATEN

Advance Praise for <u>Squirrel Inc.</u>

"Good business leaders know that there is no hard line between soft and hard, between art and science, between reality and magic. Steve Denning, a master and a leader in the value of storytelling, shows in this book how they all combine in storytelling as a leadership tool."
—Jack Grayson, chairman, and Carla O'Dell, president,
American Productivity & Quality Center (APQC)

"Storytelling is one of the most important ways of changing or reinforcing an organization's culture. Individuals who understand the power of storytelling are well on their way to becoming tomorrow's leaders. Steve Denning is a master of storytelling, and *Squirrel Inc.* is must reading for every business leader."
—Rory L. Chase, managing director, Teleos—The KNOW Network,
and editor, *Journal of Knowledge Management*

"This clever fable about *Squirrel Inc.* is a unique look at leadership and the magical power of narrative—the skill of telling the right story at the right time. While spinning his own enjoyable, highly readable story, Denning gives corporate executives who are in the process of transforming their own organizations tools to crack tough business nuts along the challenging path from vision to results."
—Melinda J. Bickerstaff, vice president, knowledge management,
Bristol-Myers Squibb Company

"*Squirrel Inc.* is invaluable because the formulas for 'situation storytelling' are revealed in a clear and concise manner, and can be immediately applied. Proven techniques are aligned with seven different situations reoccurring in business, in our communities, and our personal lives. The question is not whether storytelling successfully communicates knowledge or can persuade individuals into action, but rather if the appropriate level of passion and the correct storytelling techniques have been applied."
—Steven Wieneke, lead knowledge asset manager,
General Motors Corporation

"Unlike a lot of 'moral tales' this one has serious purpose and avoids the trivialization of the genre in recent years; it is practical and controversial in all the right ways."

— Dave Snowden, director, Cynefin Centre, IBM Global Services

"What a wonderful story of growth and development! As we learn about this community of squirrels called Squirrel Inc., we are taught about the ways that we interact with others. We learn the principles of leadership and how to apply them through different types of stories in a nonthreatening way. In the process, we learn about ourselves. This is the best book on leadership that I have read since *Watership Down* so many years ago."

— Robert H. Buckman, former CEO, Buckman Laboratories, and president, Applied Knowledge Group

"*Squirrel Inc.* is a fascinating book about leadership and change and the role of narrative in both. Told as a fable through the dialogue of a community of squirrels, the narrative keeps your attention, leading you to learn about some of those indescribable qualities of leadership that actually inspire others to follow. I was particularly captivated by the section on leadership and resilience and would highly recommend this book to anyone who is interested the true nature of leadership."

— Gayle Holtzinger, former knowledge manager, Shell Exploration and Production Co.

"*Squirrel Inc.* is the best book I have read on the subject of how to take the art of storytelling and make a real impact on the life of a company. Moreover, it's an engaging read from cover to cover, filled with useful ideas that you can immediately apply to real business challenges. While the setting is the fictitious world of squirrels, you won't fail to see a little of yourself and the heroes and villains of your own organization who daily fight to influence and change the hearts and minds of decision makers, staff, and the consumers you serve."

— Richard Stone, president, StoryWork Institute

"Many of us in KM since the early days, circa 1995, are engineers—analytical and technical. When I first heard about storytelling in the KM context, first popularized by Steve, I was more than doubtful. Wrong! Storytelling has emerged as one of the proven techniques in the KM Body of Knowledge (KMBOK™), a requirement for KMPro's KM Certification. Steve is the father of storytelling for KM, and his early approaches were taught to certificants as basic communication techniques. His new insights, leveraging storytelling for effective leadership, will be required reading for future KM leaders."

—Douglas Weidner, executive director, KMPro Learning Center CKO, Knowledge & Innovation Management Professional Society (KMPro)

"As a storytelling professional I consider *Squirrel Inc.* to be the premier resource for conveying the power of narrative in organizations today. It clearly articulates the distinctive attributes of effective storytelling, according to intent . . . perhaps the most useful way to approach the subject. This is the best thing I have read on effective organizational storytelling."

—Seth Kahan, organizational community specialist

"I couldn't put *Squirrel Inc.* down! Steve Denning, with brilliant writing and creativity, has demonstrated the natural dynamic and beauty of integrating the imagination of the right brain with the container and analytic framework of the left brain. In doing so, Steve has demonstrated the power of story and why it works! Steve Denning has woven a story—that becomes our own—and in doing so, he is revolutionizing how organizations will succeed in the year 2004 and beyond! Reading *Squirrel Inc.* will simultaneously spur the imagination and hone the understanding of anyone who wants to be effective and fulfilled, whether at work or at play."

—Lynne Feingold, organizational consultant

"This book is something new. Nestled in what appears to be a simple story are elements of deep management concepts served up with new life and insights. Steve Denning blends story practice with management theory and draws you into both with subtle ease—one might even say, sleight of hand. Drawing from his own life experience—the greatest teacher of management—he has turned it into an engaging story of stories. I loved most that the characters seem every bit real and consistent, right to the end. They leave you thinking, 'This could have happened!'"

—Madelyn Blair, CEO, Pelerei Inc.

"During my seventeen years as CEO of a landscape construction company, I struggled to find ways to increase morale, imbue our corporate ethos, and energize our staff. Toward that end, I ran workshops, hired industry consultants, and talked a blue streak. But I never thought about storytelling. As I read Steve Denning's theories, equally simple as clever, I felt sad for not bringing such an effective set of ideas into my company. What a positive effect they would surely have had."

—K. D. Solit, former president, Spring Gardens, Inc.

"Unique in describing how storytelling can be used as an effective leadership and organization change tool, *Squirrel Inc.* opens up a whole new field that has been largely ignored. A must fun-read for every business leader."

—Michel Pommier, Chad Cameroon Pipeline Projects,
HQ Coordinator, World Bank

"*Squirrel Inc.* takes organizational storytelling to the next level. As a professional storyteller working in the corporate environment, I found that it articulates simply, effectively, and instructively the most important aspects of storytelling within organizations. The thing I found most useful was the outlining of the seven highest forms of organizational storytelling and all the caveats.

I believe it is an essential tool for every storyteller wanting to take the leap into the choppy waters of 'Corporania,' as well as for story champions within organizations. While stories can't solve all organizational issues, they can make the journey more enjoyable."

—Carol Russell, organizational consultant

"When I realized, deep down, that analysis, however brilliant, explanations, however thorough, and reasons, however logical, would all leave things just as they were before, *Squirrel Inc.* showed me—clearly—another way."

—Larry Forster, oil industry change agent

"Fresh from his success in *The Springboard,* Steve provides valuable insights and guidelines to change leaders who can use the power of storytelling in the challenging tasks of persuading, influencing, and convincing."

—Sanjay Swarup, senior knowledge management specialist

SQUIRREL INC.

SQUIRREL INC.

A FABLE OF LEADERSHIP
THROUGH STORYTELLING

Stephen Denning

JOSSEY-BASS
A Wiley Imprint
www.josseybass.com

Copyright © 2004 by John Wiley & Sons, Inc. All rights reserved.

Published by Jossey-Bass
A Wiley Imprint
989 Market Street, San Francisco, CA 94103-1741   www.josseybass.com

Jossey-Bass books and products are available through most bookstores. To contact Jossey-Bass directly call our Customer Care Department within the U.S. at 800-956-7739, outside the U.S. at 317-572-3986, or fax 317-572-4002.

Jossey-Bass also publishes its books in a variety of electronic formats. Some content that appears in print may not be available in electronic books.

Text design by Paula Goldstein

Library of Congress Cataloging-in-Publication Data

Denning, Stephen.
  Squirrel Inc. : a fable of leadership through storytelling / Stephen Denning.-1st ed.
    p. cm.
  Includes bibliographical references.
  ISBN 0-7879-7371-8 (alk. paper)
  1. Communication in organizations. 2. Storytelling. 3. Leadership. 4. Organizational change. 5. Organizational learning. I. Title: Leadership through storytelling. II. Title.
  HD30.3.D462 2004
  658.4'092-dc22

                                                      2004000686

Printed in the United States of America
FIRST EDITION

HB Printing   10 9 8 7 6 5 4 3 2 1

CONTENTS

ix

PART TWO

After the success of her story with the managing
committee of Squirrel Inc., Diana joins employees to
explore other ways in which storytelling can help
address the challenges the firm is facing.

Whyse shows how storytelling can enhance
communication in corporate environments
by communicating who you are.

Hester shows how storytelling can be used to get
individuals working together. She presents
five steps to craft a story for nurturing a community.

Mark shows how stories that are told and retold in a
organization, particularly about the organization's
leaders, transmit the organization's values.

7 Mocha's Story:
How to Use Storytelling to Tame the Grapevine   79

Mocha shows how humor can be used to harness the
power of the informal network of communication in
an organization and to tame the grapevine by neutralizing rumors and bad news.

8 Howe's Story:
How to Use Storytelling to Share Knowledge   89

Howe shows how the sharing of knowledge takes
place through a particular kind of narrative.

9 Sandra's Story:
How to Use Storytelling to Create a Future   101

Sandra shows how future stories—visions, business
models, scenarios—help organizations move
into the future. Meanwhile Howe reveals some
unexpected developments within Squirrel Inc.

10 Howe Upsets the Acorns:
How Individuals and Organizations React to Change   115

The discussion in the bar now turns to what will
happen next at Squirrel Inc. Will the old way
of doing business triumph? Or will Squirrel Inc.
carry through with the change? The characters
explore these and other possibilities.

PART THREE

As the continuing tale of Squirrel Inc. unfolds,
the characters encounter a variety of surprises
and Diana goes on a journey.

We learn the impact of storytelling on Squirrel Inc.
and on Diana herself.

The nature, form, and purpose of seven
high-value kinds of organizational
storytelling are compared, in a table.

PREFACE

For all that narrative is one of our evident delights,
it is serious business.
—JEROME BRUNER

This book deals with leadership. It's about how you can use the magic of narrative to lead—from wherever you are—and to handle the principal challenges facing all leaders today:

- How do you persuade people to change?
- How do you get people working together?
- How do you share knowledge?
- How do you tame the grapevine?
- How do you communicate who you are?
- How do you transmit values?
- How do you lead people into the future?

These are among the most difficult—and significant—leadership challenges. To deal with them, there are few other usable tools.

Of the thousands of books published on the subject of leadership, only a few have hinted at the connection between leadership and storytelling. Even those writers who made a beginning dealt with storytelling as a peripheral issue. None grasped the centrality of narrative to leadership and communication or systematically spelt out its multifaceted dimensions and methods.[1]

Here—finally—are leadership tools that actually work.

In my interactions with executives in scores of large organizations, I have seen how easily and quickly people can enhance their natural storytelling capacity, once they grasp that storytelling is not some kind of primitive toy that needs to be replaced by the sleek computer-guided instruments of modern analytical thinking. Storytelling is in fact at the core of the significant activities of every modern corporation, as well as at the center of everything we do in public and private life. The ability to tell the right story at the right time is emerging as an essential leadership skill for coping with, and getting business results in, the turbulent world of the twenty-first century. It's also a critical capacity for personal interaction and happiness with family and friends.

A recent Booz Allen review concludes that "perhaps the most powerful role of stories today is to ignite and drive changes in management policy and practices."[2] Stories that spark change—springboard stories—were introduced in my book *The Springboard: How Storytelling Ignites Action in Knowledge-Era Organizations* (2000), which tells the remarkable story of transformational change in the World Bank. This refreshingly different message about leading is now spreading throughout the world. In this new book:

• Part One (Chapters One and Two) gives detailed advice on how to craft and perform a story that can spark transformational change in an organization.

- Part Two (Chapters Three through Ten) shows how to deploy six other kinds of storytelling of high value in an organizational context. Each of the chapters from Four through Nine demonstrates and explains how one of these six kinds of story is crafted and told.
- Part Three (Chapters Eleven and Twelve) illustrates the impact of storytelling on our work and personal lives.

After writing *The Springboard* I noticed that storytelling is important not only for leaders sparking a change but for anyone who needs to tell an organization's story or work with a team toward a vision or share knowledge or harness the rumor mill. I saw how different narrative objectives had different narrative patterns associated with them. I observed how using the wrong form of story for a particular purpose generally led to an unsuccessful result. And so I set about creating the tale of Squirrel Inc. to show how understanding the different narrative patterns can help people find and tell a story that gets them to their objective.

What Sort of Storytelling Are We Talking About?

Needless to say, when this book talks of storytelling, it isn't talking about fairy tales or the traditional stories that are told to children. It's talking about the sorts of stories that are told every day in organizations throughout the world by busy executives to achieve real-world objectives.

Some of the stories that occur in organizations are close cousins of traditional stories, which of course have a long history. The principles of traditional storytelling were described more than two thousand years ago by the Greek philosopher Aristotle in his *Poetics*. These are stories that have a beginning, a middle, and an ending, and a plot with characters that combines a reversal and a recognition; the storyteller visualizes the action and feels with the characters so that listeners immerse themselves in the world of the story.[3] Examples of such fictions are the tales of Ovid, Scheherazade, Boccaccio, and Mark Twain; the hero's journey described by Joseph Campbell; and the plots featured in the popular cinema.[4] Traditional stories are still relevant to some purposes in a modern organization, such as communicating who you are (discussed in Chapter Four) or getting people working together (Chapter Five).[5]

This book is also about other types of narratives identified by practitioners who have looked beyond the principles of traditional storytelling. Rather than examining how stories *ought* to be told, they have studied the narratives that are *actually* being told in organizations in terms of the purposes they serve and the impact they have. Although nontraditional stories don't always comply with Aristotle's principles of storytelling, they include some of the most valuable forms of storytelling in a modern organization. Among them are springboard stories that communicate complex ideas and spark action (discussed in Chapters One and Two), stories that tame the grapevine (Chapter Seven), stories that share knowledge (Chapter Eight), and stories that lead people into the future (Chapter Nine).[6]

The tale of Squirrel Inc. thus deals with both traditional and nontraditional storytelling in organizations. It sets out to clarify which kind of story makes sense in which context and why. It aims at both demonstrating and explaining the differences, so that readers will be more likely to find and tell stories that will accomplish their objectives.

Why Squirrels?

Squirrel Inc. is a fable in which the characters are squirrels. Why squirrels?

When I came to write this book, I had to consider how I could best communicate the various kinds of stories, their specific uses in modern organizations, and their relevant similarities and differences. I quickly discovered that conveying an understanding of seven types of stories across four or five different dimensions represented a level of complexity not well adapted to textbook-style presentation.

As a proponent of storytelling to communicate complex ideas, I found it natural to turn to narrative. Over the centuries animal fables have successfully communicated complex messages to diverse audiences. Aesop and La Fontaine did it with menageries of animals, Franz Kafka with a cockroach, George Orwell with pigs, James Agee with cows, Daniel Quinn with a gorilla, and Spencer Johnson with mice.[7] This book employs squirrels.

Squirrels sparked my imagination in several ways. Some years ago I was reading that wonderful compendium of statistics known as the Harper's Index, and I noticed an oddball figure. It was the percentage of nuts that squirrels lost because they couldn't remember where they had buried them. It was a remarkably high percentage,[8] and the fact, if not the exact number, stuck in my mind. Later, as I watched families of squirrels run about my garden, I thought of the huge numbers of nuts that they were continually losing. What would happen, I thought, if one day the squirrels decided to change? So this book tells the story of the transformation of an imaginary organization called Squirrel Inc. from a nut-burying to a nut-storing organization. We follow the transformation as it goes from an improbability (Chapter One) to a possibility (Chapter Two) to a probability (Chapter Three) to a lost opportunity (Chapter Nine), and then there is yet another turn of events (Chapters Eleven and Twelve).

The density of squirrels in Washington, D.C., is among the highest in the world. I have done much of my writing there, in a room that looks out over several gardens. From my window I could at one time see a large old mulberry tree, and it was remarkable how many squirrels played on its long, wide horizontal branches. From time to time I would look up from my writing and see countless pairs of squirrels gamboling and frolicking on this tree with such evident pleasure my spirits would lift. It was obvious that the branches of the mulberry tree made a wonderful playground for them. Then one day I looked out the window and saw no mulberry tree! My neighbors had without warning cut it down. Because a mulberry tree is a messy thing in a city garden, I understood their action, but I was shocked on behalf of the squirrels. How would they feel when they found that their mulberry tree had been cut down? The mulberry tree story plays a major role in Part Two of this book.[9]

Squirrel Inc. introduces a cast of furry characters who together learn the art of storytelling in their quest to overcome obstacles, generate enthusiasm and teamwork, share important knowledge, and ultimately lead their company into a new era of success and significance. Together, the squirrels discover that the ability to tell the right story at the right time can have a pivotal impact on the success or failure of any major change effort.

Among the characters that you will meet are

A *bartender*, who hosts a nectar bar in the vicinity of Squirrel Inc.

Diana, an up-and-coming executive at Squirrel Inc. who discovers the power of stories to spark action

Whyse, an advocate of storytelling that communicates who you are

Hester, who uses storytelling to get people working together

Mark, who discusses storytelling to transmit values

Mocha, who shows how humor can be used to tame the grapevine

Howe, who deploys storytelling to share knowledge

Sandra, who pursues storytelling to lead into the future

Ted, the director of public relations at Squirrel Inc.

Apart from the bartender, all these characters work for Squirrel Inc.

What Sort of an Organization Is Squirrel Inc.?

Squirrel Inc. is an imaginary organization with all too familiar difficulties. Once it was among the corporate elite. It was doing well by any standard. Its profits grew steadily over a sustained period. Its stock was selling at a high multiple of earnings. Its management was widely admired as a model.

But times have changed. The marketplace has changed. Squirrel Inc.'s revenues are stagnating. Its market share is eroding. Its once-admired management practices no longer cut the mustard. Once Squirrel Inc. could do no wrong in investors' eyes; now it can do hardly anything right.

Its executive team is working the same long hours, but the firm is no longer getting the extraordinary results it once got.

Squirrel Inc. is not a bad company. It isn't involved in systematic illegality or downright fraud, like Enron. It's trying to do the right thing. Its managers are not intentionally cheating or stealing. They are not crooks. But Squirrel Inc. is not getting the results it needs to flourish.

Nor has Squirrel Inc. been blindsided by some unexpected event that could not have been foreseen. As happens in many actual companies, the reasons for its decline have been staring its executives in the face for some time. The very habits and practices that made the firm successful in the past have become shackles that are inhibiting innovation and hampering the changes that need to be made.

Squirrel Inc.'s executives are in varying degrees aware of the reasons for the firm's decline. Yet there is no agreement as to what to do, even if, as in many real-life cases, it is obvious to anyone outside the organization what ought to be done. For Squirrel Inc., change is irresistible but the organization seems immovable.[10]

Thus, like many organizations today, Squirrel Inc. desperately needs leadership. As it happens, this is a challenge that narrative techniques are well adapted to handle. The tale of Squirrel Inc. is about the use of storytelling as a set of tools to lift the firm out of its downward trajectory, to get individuals working together, to help to regenerate innovation, and to move the firm forward into the future.

So if you're interested in using storytelling as a tool for leading, in understanding the unexpectedly large role of organizational storytelling in the modern world, or simply in following an entertaining story, go ahead: read, learn, and enjoy! I hope you have as much fun reading this tale as I had writing it.

March 2004   STEPHEN DENNING
Washington, D.C.

SQUIRREL INC.

Part One

One can't make a new heaven
and earth with "facts."
—HENRY MILLER

Chapter One

SQUIRREL INC.

How to Craft a Story to Spark Organizational Change

Estimated percentage of nuts that squirrels lose
because they forget where they put them: 50
—THE HARPER'S INDEX BOOK

I t is ten-thirty in the morning when she climbs for the first time into my tavern high up in the old oak tree on 44th Street. I observe that her fur is smooth and perfectly groomed. I've never seen her in here before, or indeed anywhere in these green and leafy trees, but from the way she comes in with her tail very straight and twitching, she is visibly with it, totally today. She asks for a double-fermented rose nectar, with a twist, shaken but not stirred, and then insists that I use a different woodcup, with a thinner lip and chilled for no less than a minute. Even something as simple as a drink involves a mass of planning—typical Squirrel Inc. Yet I also sense something else hidden beneath her furry façade. It's faint but, for a wizened old bartender like myself, unmistakable — something haunting, half-formed, incomplete.

She's carrying off the appearance of being a calm and collected Squirrel Inc. exec with all the pieces of her existence interlocking in a carefully planned pattern. But a Squirrel Inc. exec doesn't climb into a dark, dapple-lit tavern like mine high up in an old oak tree on a bright sunny spring morning, alone, and order a double-fermented nectar unless something is up with the plan of her well-ordered life.

But there's no sense rushing things. It's still early and the tavern is practically deserted. I get her the fermented nectar and fix her fresh hickory nuts. I go on cleaning the wood-cups, getting everything ready for the usual lunchtime rush, casual-like but hovering all the time in her vicinity, so that when she's ready for it, she can get what all squirrels are looking for when they come into my tavern — unintrusive company, a sympathetic ear, contact with some other living thing.

Years ago you wouldn't have seen a female squirrel alone in here at all, or if you had, you'd have known that she hadn't exactly come here for a drink. But times have changed. The squirrel workforce is now full of females clambering their way up managerial ladders and smashing into glass ceilings with alarming frequency. I see all types in here — male, female, gray, brown, black, all shades, all shapes, you name it. Why should I discriminate? These are difficult times for squirrels. Somewhere, there has to be a place of respite, an oasis where bruised egos can find succor, comfort, a substitute for love.

She finishes her double-ferment a little too quickly.

"Another?" I suggest. I have to stay in business too, you know.

"Why not?" she replies.

Last night's rain has washed and refreshed the atmosphere. A breeze carrying smells of wet grass and fresh earth is blowing gently though the tavern.

"Great day, huh?" I prompt as I hand her the second woodcup of fermented nectar.

"I wish," she whispers as she cradles her drink.

Pause.

"Difficulties?" I venture.

"Big time," she replies.

"Happens."

"Not to me, it doesn't," she says. "Not to *the* rising star of Squirrel Inc."

Why am I not surprised?

"Here I am," she continues. "The hope of the firm's future. The one that's beaten every nutty goal they've ever given her. The one that knows what to do when the firm is in crisis. The one with the idea that will enable it to survive."

"And?"

"No one's listening," she says. "It's as if I no longer exist. Suddenly I'm an outcast. They see me coming and they run the other way. The thing is, they're not going to survive as an organization if they don't listen. I know I'm right."

"Right."

"I've just come from a meeting," she says. "I'd done all the numbers, and the rates of return were amazing. I'd put together a presentation. All the right slides. I thought it was straightforward. But they just looked dazed."

"You gave them reasons?"

"I gave them reasons till they came out of my spleen.

5

They're simply not listening. My idea is too strange, too disruptive, too different."

"Pity," I say as she sails through her second drink.

"Someone told me that you may be able to help."

"Me?"

"Skip said you'd know what to do."

"Skip?"

"A friend," she says. "He said you'd come up with something new. Something old that's being put to a new use. What did he mean?"

"I guess he means Dio."

"Dio?"

"A squirrel," I say. "Used to hang out here."

"I've got to talk to him."

"Actually this is a she," I say. "She's on the road a lot."

"I need to speak to her."

"Not sure that's possible," I say. "She hasn't been here in a while."

"There must be a way," she says agitatedly.

"Not that I know of."

She takes a pull of her double-ferment.

"I mean, who is she? What is she?" She stares at me.

"Dio? She taught me all I know. Got to the top of one company and was about to be thrown out. And then she figured out how to get back in the game. Used to be here all the time telling us how she did it. Now she's moved on."

"Why?"

"Fresh woods. New pastures. How would I know?"

"No need to get your fur ruffled," she says.

"I'm perfectly calm," I say.

"But you heard her talk?"

6

"Yep."

"More than once?"

"All the time," I say, arranging some acorns.

"You followed what she was saying?"

"I know it backwards," I say.

"Skip said it was a miracle," she says.

"Miracles don't exist, my friend."

"I mean, just try. What would Dio say to me if she were here right now?"

She looks at me with those big round squirrel eyes and I feel again that incompleteness. "Many things," I say.

"For instance?"

"Suppose I told you it costs nothing and is very easy and natural?"

"Then I wouldn't believe you," she says. "How could it possibly work?"

"Suppose I told you it's something that's hard-wired into our brains at birth?"

"I'd ask myself what you'd been smoking."

"Did you ever try telling a story?" I ask.

"Why would I do that?"

"Because a story can communicate a new idea quickly, easily, and naturally."

"Not in Squirrel Inc.," she says.

"Why not?"

"Stories aren't serious," she says. "Squirrel Inc. is. It's modern. It's analytic. It's sharp. It's focused on profits. It's bottom-line. It doesn't mess around. No emotional mush. No touchy-feely stuff. Squirrel Inc. would never go for anything like that."

"Did you ever actually *try* a story?" I ask.

7

"As a matter of fact, I did," she says. "One meeting, I described what the future would be like."

"Result?"

"They said it would never happen here. Perhaps in some other company, but not in Squirrel Inc."

"Maybe," I say, "there's another way to tell the story."

"What do you mean?" she asks.

"Dio said there are different purposes in telling a story, and for each purpose you tell the story in a different way. Maybe you told the story in the wrong way to achieve your goal."

"It doesn't matter," she says. "I know a story won't work."

"Right."

The mockingbirds are in full song now as she nurses her double-ferment.

"But you've heard Dio talk," she says. "She knew how to communicate a new idea and get everyone into action."

"If you say so."

"If I don't get the big idea across," she says, "I'm going to be roadkill."

"So what *is* the big idea?" I say. "How *are* you going to save Squirrel Inc.?"

"Simple," she says, and smiles. "Squirrel Inc. has always been a company that helps squirrels bury nuts. That's not going to work in the future. The nuts keep getting lost. It's got to become a nut-storing company."

"Going from nut burying to nut storing is a pretty big transition," I say.

"It's too much for them," she says. "Squirrels have always buried nuts as a matter of instinct. But it's not going to work anymore. Humans keep digging up their gardens. The

8

nut-loss rate is just too great. It worked wonders for us, all those years. But now those years are over."

"Your idea is pretty clear?" I say.

"Couldn't be clearer," she says.

"Then you're halfway home. Most of the time, Dio would say, the problem in getting an idea across is right there in the first step."

"What's that?"

"Getting clear on the purpose," I say. "What's the change you're aiming for? It sounds like the easiest thing to be clear about. It should be obvious. So many squirrels come in here, all upset, but when you pin them down and get them to say what change they want, they don't really know. They haven't thought it through. So you're way ahead of the game. You've already got a clear idea of what change you're trying to make. You've already taken the first step."

STEP ONE

Be clear about what change you're trying to make.

She looks at me intently. "OK, wise guy, what's the second step?"

"You really want to do this?"

"Yes," she says, "I do."

"Then think of an incident."

"Think of an incident?"

"Exactly. Think of an example where this has already happened successfully, even in part."

"You mean, make something up?"

"No. That's not going to work. You need a true story. It's the truth of the story that springs the listener to a new level

9

of understanding. I'm talking about a real-life incident where this actually happened."

"There isn't any."

"Think harder!"

STEP TWO
Think of an incident, a story, where the change has already happened.

"This idea is new for Squirrel Inc.," she says. "It's a nut-burying company, not a nut-storing company."

"Has any other company done it?"

"Not that I know of."

"You mean no squirrel has ever set about storing acorns rather than burying them? Ever?"

"Nope."

"Not even outside the company?"

"Well," she says, "there were a couple of squirrels I once heard about."

"Tell me more."

"I know a squirrel called Skip."

"So I gather."

"Skip and I were going together, but then he went to live in another city."

"And?"

"Well, he told me about some squirrels there. They experimented with storing acorns, and everyone said they were crazy."

"Did it work for them?"

"It worked beautifully," she says, "for part of the winter. They sat back and relaxed and ate their stores of acorns. But they didn't store enough. They ran out in January."

"So there *was* a case where this actually happened."

"That's what Skip told me."

"And it worked?"

"In part," she says. "Not as well as it might have if they'd stored enough acorns and had the proper storage conditions. But, yes, in part, it worked."

"What do you know about the squirrels who tried it?"

"Skip said they were a mixed bag. A new-age group."

"What else do you know about them?"

"They were a wild bunch," she says. "You know, doing odd stuff, except for one nifty squirrel who focused on hickory nuts because they lasted longer. He made it through to February. His name was Timmy."

"Timmy?"

"The only normal one in the bunch, according to Skip."

"And he almost got through the winter?"

"Not right through," she says. "According to Skip, Timmy didn't store enough nuts with the proper storage conditions, so eventually he had to go out looking for buried nuts. He does the books for some big company."

STEP THREE
Tell the story from the point of view of a single protagonist who is typical of the potential audience.

"So Timmy is not too different from the squirrels you're trying to convince in Squirrel Inc?"

"Maybe," she says.

"Where did this happen?" I ask.

"The Windy City," she says.

"When?" I ask.

"Last winter," she says. "But I don't get it. What's your point?"

11

"What we're doing," I say, "is crafting a story that you can use to get Squirrel Inc. to understand the idea of storing nuts and implement it. Giving the date and place signals to the listener's brain that this really did happen."

"But Timmy is only one squirrel," she says, "and even he didn't get through the winter. My idea is about millions of squirrels, all of them getting through the winter by storing nuts. How can a story about a single squirrel convince anyone?"

"You'd be surprised," I say.

"Think about it," she says. "As evidence, a single squirrel is insignificant. Now, if I had a survey showing that lots of squirrels in the Windy City were getting through the winter storing nuts, that might get some attention. But just one squirrel? And that squirrel messed up? Forget it!"

STEP FOUR

Specify the time and place where the story happened.

Just then the sun flashes through the leaves for an instant and highlights the troubled expression on her face.

"It's not the number of squirrels involved," I say. "That's thinking with only one side of your brain—the left side. Why don't you try the right side for a change?"

"What do you mean?"

"The left side of the brain analyzes things in a rational way—three threes are nine. The right side of the brain looks at things more creatively. For the right side of the brain, three threes might be nine. But they could also be three hundred and thirty-three. There's always more than one way to understand something."

"But what's in this for Squirrel Inc.?" she says. "They're only interested in the analysis. They don't give a damn about the imagination. Just the bottom line! What do they care about a bunch of mixed-up squirrels in the Windy City? *Nada. Rien. Nichts.* In Squirrel Inc., three threes are nine, *punto!* They'll never go for a story."

"That's where you're missing something," I say. "The fact is, we all tell stories. We start doing it when we're little, with our parents, our brothers and sisters, our friends. We tell stories for all sorts of purposes, unconsciously, instinctively, intuitively. We don't have to be taught how to do this. We do it naturally."

"Exactly," she says. "This stuff is for babies."

"That's what we're told when we go to school," I say. "We're told, 'OK, children, now you're going to put aside your toys and your stories. Now you're going to study the significant things—math, algebra, geometry, physics, chemistry.' And so we forget about storytelling."

"But that's just school."

"The same thing happens when we join an organization like Squirrel Inc. It's all about analysis and abstractions. But what do we do after one of these exhausting, boring lessons at school or the even more boring meetings in an organization? We rush outside and . . . ?"

"We relax," she says.

"But how?" I say. "We tell stories. We tell stories with our friends, our colleagues, our family. Anyone who'll listen. Why? We find it energizing. We find it refreshing. We can do it all day. We can do it all night. Even when we're asleep, we dream in stories. We can't get enough of it. Storytelling is our very nature. We've just pretended to ourselves that we're

13

something that we're not. And the squirrels at Squirrel Inc. are no different. They might *say* they're not interested in a story, but if you tell them a story, they'll listen."

"But we don't have a story."

"Yes, we do," I say. "Just think:

STEP FIVE
Make sure the story embodies the change idea, or if it doesn't, extrapolate the change. from the story.

"Last winter in the Windy City a squirrel named Timmy did something different. Instead of burying nuts and searching for them when he was hungry, he spent the fall gathering nuts and storing them in his tree hollow. Timmy was able to relax with his family nearly all winter, safe in knowing he had a full supply of nuts."

"But Timmy didn't get through the winter that way," she says. "He didn't store enough nuts."

"No problem," I say. "Here's what you do. You tell Timmy's story up to February and then say:

"'Let's imagine. Let's extrapolate.' Imagine if Timmy had been able to store enough nuts. He would have had a supply of food for the whole winter."

"But they'll say it didn't happen," she says. "You just told me the story has to be true."

"The initial incident needs to be true," I say, "because it's the truth of the story that snaps the listeners out of their complacency. If you tell them a purely imaginary story, then they'll say, 'This will never happen here!'"

"That's right. That's what they said."

"They're still using the left side of their brain," I say. "But now you can say, 'Listen! I'm not making this up. This actually happened!' When you've got the listeners following the story, imagining what actually happened, they're using the right side of the brain. Then you can push their imaginations a step further. You can get them to extrapolate. You can say, 'Just think what could have happened if the story had continued into the future.' You anchor the listeners' imagination initially in reality. And then they'll follow that story into the future."

STEP SIX

In telling the story, make clear what would have happened without the change idea.

"But will they see the point? Will they see why this story is different?"

"You make them see it," I say, "by pointing out what would have happened if Timmy hadn't been implementing the change idea."

"How do I do that?" she says.

"Simple. You say:

"Just imagine how Timmy the squirrel would have spent his winter if he hadn't had his store of nuts, scraping and grubbing around, getting frustrated most of the time. Nothing being where he'd left it.

"In this way, you remind your listeners how most squirrels now spend their winters. You highlight how different Timmy's winter was from the typical squirrel winter."

"How does the story sound now?" she asks.

"Why don't you try it?" I say.

"You think I can?"

"Of course. Imagine I'm a manager at Squirrel Inc."

"All right. Here goes.

"I have a good friend, Skip, who lives out in the Windy City. Skip knew a whole colony of squirrels out there. They all lived in a big willow tree out by a river. Normally they spent their winters burying nuts and searching for them, scraping around, getting disappointed a lot of the time. Nothing was where they'd left it, and often they were hungry.

"Last winter they decided to do something different. They'd heard it was going to be a really cold winter. You know, they don't call it the Windy City for nothing. The wind slices through there like a knife. So they spent the fall gathering nuts and stored them in a tree hollow. They were able to relax with their families with a full store of nuts. That got them up to January and then they ran out. But if they'd been able to store more nuts, they would have been able to have a supply of food for the whole winter."

She looks at me. "How did I do?"

"Great!" I say. The double-ferments have given her energy. "But there's still work to be done."

"Oh?"

"It had a lot of good points, but we can make it better."

"How's that?" she says, her whiskers now bristling.

"Remember what I said about the single protagonist? A single hero or heroine that the listener can connect with?"

"Yes."

"Well," I say, "who's your single protagonist?"

"Skip."

"Did Skip store any nuts?"

"No," she says. "He's the squirrel who told me about doing it."

"Exactly. The person who told you the story doesn't interest the listeners. When you start out talking about Skip, they might think that the story is about Skip. But it's not about Skip. It's about squirrels storing nuts. Skip just confuses the listeners and distracts them. We've got to get Skip offstage. Let's think for a minute. Who *is* your single protagonist?"

"I went one better than a single protagonist," she says. "I gave you a whole colony of squirrels. Surely the more squirrels we have, the more convincing the story, right?"

STEP SEVEN
Strip the story of unnecessary detail.

"Not necessarily! You're thinking with the left side of your brain again. In matters of evidence, the more witnesses you have, the stronger the testimony. But in storytelling, you're not using the weight of the evidence. You're operating on the right side of the brain, sparking the imagination and so getting the listener to think what it might be like spending the whole winter relaxing and drawing on a store of nuts. The thing is, it's easier to identify with a single squirrel than with a whole group of squirrels. Just give us Timmy. Get your listeners to identify with Timmy."

"I see," she says. "What else?"

She's taking it pretty well, as I give her more hickory nuts.

"Too much detail," I say.

"Isn't that how you tell a story? Sights and sounds. How cold the wind was. Living in a willow tree by the river. That sort of thing. Make the listener feel what it was like?"

"You're right when it comes to a story for entertainment. But not when you're telling a story for a purpose. The mechanism is different. Stories for entertainment immerse the listener in the storyteller's story. The idea is to absorb the listeners so completely in the story that they think about nothing else. When you're using storytelling as a tool, it works just the opposite. You're not trying to absorb the listener in your story."

"Why not?"

"You're trying to spark a new story in the listener's mind. You're talking about a bunch of squirrels in the Windy City, but you don't want the listeners thinking about them too much. Instead, you want the listeners to be thinking about their own situation. You want them thinking, 'Hey, that's pretty interesting! We could do that! Suppose we started storing nuts instead of burying them? We could relax all winter instead of scurrying around searching.'"

"So the listeners create their own story?"

"Right. The listeners start crafting a new story in their own minds. They start to invent the change idea afresh. It becomes their own idea adapted to their own differing situations. And of course we all love our own ideas."

"How do you make this happen?"

"You strip the story of details that are unrelated to the change idea. You tell the story in a simplified way so that there's nothing to distract the listeners."

"Will they still be able to follow the story if I take out all the detail?"

"You leave in enough detail for them to follow the story and you delete all the rest."

"But will the story still be interesting?"

"You make it interesting in the way you tell it. You tell it with belief and feeling. It's your performance that gives the story its force. You don't need the other details."

"What else?"

"We've got to work on the ending."

"What's wrong with it?"

"Hollywood is right. It's got to have a happy ending."

"You mean, 'They lived happily ever after'?"

"Sounds corny, but guess what? It works. With a negative story, you're sadder but wiser. You learn something. But as you think about the negative implications of what happened, you end up in a mood of concern and worry. You don't feel like moving forward rapidly into action. In contrast, a story with a happy ending generates a feeling of gentle euphoria—the perfect state of mind to be thinking about a new future for you or your organization."

STEP EIGHT
Make sure the story has an authentically happy ending.[a]

"What does that mean for my story?" she says.

"It means that you emphasize the success in storing nuts, not the problems that had to be solved."

"Is that all?"

"One final thing," I say. "You need to nudge the listeners so that they get the point. Not in a heavy-handed way. Don't overpower them. Just provide tiny guiderails so that the listeners spring to where you want them to go. You might say:

STEP NINE

Link the story to the change idea with phrases such as "Think . . ." and "What if . . ." and "Just imagine . . ."

"What if all our squirrels used modern storage techniques? Just think of the possibilities for Squirrel Inc. if it was helping all squirrels use this technology. Imagine what a business that could be!

"The magic words are, 'Imagine . . .' or 'Just think . . .' or 'What if . . .' You invite the listeners to travel on the wings of imagination and envision a different future."

"How would that all sound?"

"How about this:

"I know we're all quite worried here at Squirrel Inc. about the decline in revenues from our nut-burying business. Unfortunately that's only going to get worse because the humans are digging up their gardens at an ever-increasing pace, so this business can only get smaller. How can Squirrel Inc. survive in these increasingly difficult conditions? What's the future going to look like?

"Well, it's going to look like today. Let me tell you about something that happened just a few months ago.

"Last winter in the Windy City, a squirrel called Timmy was facing a particularly difficult situation because gardens were being dug up all over the place. Normally he would have spent his winter scraping and searching, being disappointed most of the time. Nothing would be where he'd left it. He'd have been hungry half the winter.

"But that's not what happened to Timmy. He did something different. Instead of burying nuts and searching for them when he was hungry, he spent the fall gathering them and storing them securely in his tree hollow. Timmy was able to relax with his family and his full store of nuts right up to February.

"But just imagine if Timmy had been able to store more nuts with the proper technology: he would have had a supply of food for the whole winter.

"Imagine if all squirrels used modern storage techniques. What if Squirrel Inc. was helping millions of squirrels store their acorns and other nuts? Just think what a business that could be for Squirrel Inc."

She looks at me with a strangely twitching face. A mockingbird is imitating the robins with its song.

"I'm not the first squirrel to come in here with this kind of a problem, am I?" She looks at me quizzically. "How did you get into this?"

"My grandmother told me stories when I was young. Wonderful yarns that lasted forever. It gave me a love of storytelling that's continued through my life. After all, that's what a bartender does all day—tell and listen to stories."

"Think a story would work on Skip?"

"I thought he was in another city."

"He could always come back."

"Skip wouldn't commit?"

"How did you know?"

"Someone once said we must be willing to let go of the life we have planned so that we can have the life that is waiting for us."[1]

"What does that mean?" she asks.

The bar is starting to fill up now, and I'm going to be running my claws off before long. I tell her to come back later in the day, and I'll be happy to talk more about stories.

"Thanks," she says. "Name's Diana. I'll be back."[2]

CRAFTING A STORY TO SPARK ORGANIZATIONAL CHANGE
Guidelines

At a time when most organizations are faced with the necessity of disruptive change, leaders typically find it difficult to get those who must carry out the change not only to understand new ideas but also to start implementing them rapidly and enthusiastically. The conventional wisdom that transformational change can be catalyzed by giving people a reason to change reflects a confidence in pure reason that is as touching as it is deluded.[3]

A *springboard story* enables an audience to make a leap in understanding so as to grasp how an organization or community may change. Its impact comes not so much through transferring large amounts of information as through catalyzing understanding. A springboard story enables listeners to visualize from a story about change in one context the ideas and actions involved in implementing such a change in an analogous context. In this way the change becomes the listeners' idea.

Steps in Crafting a Springboard Story
- The leader defines the specific change idea to be implemented in the organization.

- The leader identifies an incident (either inside or outside the organization, community, or group) where the change idea was in whole or in part successfully implemented.
- The incident is narrated from the perspective of a single protagonist who is typical of the target audience.
- The story specifies when and where the incident happened.
- In telling the story, the leader ensures that the story fully embodies the change idea, extrapolating the idea from the story if necessary.
- The story makes clear what would have happened without the change idea.
- The story is stripped of any unnecessary detail.
- The story has an authentically happy ending.
- At the conclusion of the story, the leader links the story to the change idea with phrases such as "What if . . ." or "Just imagine . . ."

Caveat: a story is not the only solution for all organizational communications. For some purposes, analysis is superior. The leader marries narrative with analysis, using narrative to draw listeners inside the idea so that they understand it, while also using analysis to communicate the costs, benefits, risks, and implementation issues.

Chapter Two

DIANA TELLS HER STORY

How to Perform the Story to Spark Change

*The future is already here.
But it is very unevenly distributed.*
—WILLIAM GIBSON

I don't see Diana later that day.

Nor the next day.

Nor the day after that.

In fact three days go by, and I'm beginning to think that she's not coming back, when, late in the afternoon, in she skips with her take-no-prisoners grin in position. There's a willful spring in her step.

She sits down at the bar without saying a thing. I'd like to know how it went. But I hardly need to ask. Her body language says everything.

"Double ferment?"

"Mineral water with a twist," she says perkily.

"Are you all right?" I ask.

"Fine," she says.

I go on cleaning the woodcups.

There is silence in the bar, but in the background a cardinal is singing.

"Go on," she says finally. "Ask me!"

In performing the story the storyteller relives the story and makes it fresh.

"Ask you what?"

She glares at me. "Ask me how it went."

I continue cleaning the woodcups for a few seconds as she drinks the mineral water in a couple of swallows. I think her brain is going to burst if I don't pop the question.

"OK," I say finally. "How did it go?"

"Tremendous!" she says.

"You told a story?"

"Just like you said."

"And?"

"Suddenly they're willing to listen!"

"Surprised?"

"I told it one-on-one to my buddies," she says, "and they loved it. Then I tried it on a vice president, and he got all excited. Now I have to address the managing committee. Now what do I do?"

"Go on doing what you're already doing," I suggest.

"You really think it will work?"

"You're not going into throes of self-doubt, I hope?"

"I can't afford a gaffe," she says. "This is *the* managing committee of Squirrel Inc. Can you imagine?"

"What's the alternative?" I ask.

"I need to find a new story," she says.

"Why would you need to do that?"

"This is the CEO and all his direct reports. Think of the risk if they don't go for it. What do I do?"

"Go on telling your story?"

"I've already told it a couple of times. Everyone's getting to know it. The top expects something special."

"It's the way you tell it that makes it special."

"What do you mean?"

"You need to tell the story as if you're living it in your own mind for the first time. It's the intensity of your belief in the story that sparks the listeners to live it also. If you believe, they too will believe."

> The storyteller should try to find a story that works equally well at all levels of the organization.

"That's fine," she says. "But why not a new story?"

"Just think for a minute," I say. "If you tell one story to the bottom and another to the top, then pretty soon everyone starts asking why you're telling different stories to different people. 'Is the story she told us the truth? Or is she putting us on?' When you tell different stories, it can put your authenticity in question. If you can get a story that works with the whole organization—the top, the middle, the bottom, the front office, the back office, and so on—it's generally more effective."

"You mean I go on telling the same story forever?"

"No, not forever," I say. "But it's not the quantity of stories that matters. It's the quality. Once you find a story that works, you keep on using it."

"But if some listeners hear it over and over, won't they be bored?"

"Not necessarily," I say. "Even when they hear it a second time, or even a seventh time, it isn't necessarily a problem. Remember, this kind of story works in terms of getting the listeners to think of a new story in their own context. So, if it continues to spark a new story from the listener, it doesn't matter that the storyteller's story isn't new. So long as it elicits a new story from the listener—that's the bottom line."

> Once you find a story that works, you keep using it.

"But how can I know that? How can I tell?"

"At the time you're telling the story, you'll sense the interest of the listeners. It's afterward that you'll see the real impact."

"But how?" she says.

"You'll hear others talking about your story," I say. "You'll see action start to materialize. You'll watch the problems dissolve. If the story's working, you'll know it when you see it. There'll be spontaneous enthusiasm."

"I've seen that already," she says. "By the way, you know what my boss wants me to do?"

"What?"

"He said, 'Write it up in a memo and distribute it instead.' What do I do about that?"

"Ignore him."

"He's my boss."

"Then play along," I say. "Do whatever to humor him. Write the memo. Distribute it if it keeps him happy. But it won't have the same effect."

"How come?"

"This is not about a *story*. It's about *storytelling*. It's your interaction face-to-face with individuals that makes the difference."

> Keep in mind that it's storytelling, more than the story, that has the impact.

"Let's get back to the managing committee," she says. "Maybe I should get Timmy to come and tell the story?"

"I'm not sure about that," I say.

"Why?" she asks.

"The big risk in having Timmy tell the story is that he's so involved in the story he may lose sight of why he's telling it. I mean, do you think he could tell his story in forty-five seconds?"

"I don't know," she says.

"No way!" I say. "Just think. He's come all the way from the Windy City. He finds himself on center stage at Squirrel Inc. He's more likely to tell it in forty-five minutes than in forty-five seconds. His interest is in the Windy City and everything that he did there. He's so interested in *his own* story, he'll think everyone else is interested too. The

> Recognize that the protagonist may not be the best person to tell the story.

challenge is to say just enough to spark a new story in the mind of the listener."

"I see."

"Another mineral water?" I ask.

"Thanks," she says. "But what if my story misfires?"

"It won't. Not if you tell it right."

"But how do I tell it right? The whole thing is terrific so far, don't get me wrong, but when I tell the story, somehow it doesn't sound as powerful. How do I get to your level of telling?"

"Practice, practice, practice. And again, more practice."

"Where?" she says. "And how?"

Recognize that you become a better storyteller through practice.

"Anywhere. With anyone who'll listen. Storytelling is a performance art. Observing what actually works with your audience is key. It's worked for you so far, right?"

"It did misfire one time," she says.

"Tell me about it."

"I talked to a group and no one listened."

"That can happen."

"Thanks a lot!"

"Just compare one misfire with what you were doing before. *Nothing* was working before. No one was listening. Now you're generally having success. You can't expect 100 percent triumph. If most of your audiences get it, then you're way ahead of the game."

"How can I prevent a misfire?" she says.

"You frame the story."

"Frame it?"

"Typically audiences aren't listening to begin with," I say. "It may look like they're listening. They're physically present. They're staring straight at you. But their minds are somewhere else entirely. They're sitting there thinking, 'How do I get out of here? How do I get back to my work and deal with the stuff that's piling up?' They're not listening to you at all."

"So what do I do?" she asks.

"One thing to do," I say, "is to talk about *their* agenda. There must be something on their minds. So you talk about that. You remind them of what they're worried about. And you continue: 'But it's actually worse than you think. Let me tell you how bad the situation really is!' You describe their issue in terms that are starker than anything they've ever heard before. Suddenly they're listening. In fact they're riveted on what you're saying, because this is more than interesting. Now they're ripe for the story to spark action. Remember how I began the story with you a few days ago?"

"Not really," she says.

"It went something like this:

"I know we're all worried here at Squirrel Inc. about the decline in revenues from our nut-burying business. Unfortunately that's only going to get worse. The humans are digging up the gardens at an ever-increasing pace, so our business can only get smaller. What's the future going to look like? What will Squirrel Inc. have to do to flourish in these grimmer conditions we'll be facing?"

> Recognize that initially the audience may not be listening and that you may need to get their attention.

> Talking about the listeners' problems is one way of getting their attention.

31

"You talk to the listeners in their terms?" she says.

"That's one way to do it," I say. "Another way to get their attention is to make yourself vulnerable. You tell the truth about something to which you have unique access — namely, yourself and your life story."

"Why would anyone be interested in that?" she says. "Squirrel Inc. isn't a touchy-feely company."

"You'd be surprised," I say. "You start to reveal things about yourself that make the audience think, 'Hey, this isn't just a messenger with no views of her own. This is an individual with a history. She has personality. She has character. She's seems to be leveling with us. Maybe she's telling the truth.'"

> Another way of getting the listeners' attention is by telling the truth about yourself.

"You want me to expose myself?"

"I agree, you need to be careful. You might say some things that could actually set you back. But revealing something vulnerable can make the listeners think of you as an individual, someone worth listening to."

"I see," she says, drawing on her mineral water. "How much framing will I need for the managing committee?"

"It depends on whether they're listening. If they're listening at the start, then you begin with the story right away."

"But what if they don't want a story? They didn't ask for a story. They asked for a strategic plan."

"You don't say up front you're going to tell a story. In a modern corporation that can set off alarm bells. Instead, you say: 'Let me tell you about something that happened last winter.' And if their interest is piqued, they will want to find out what happened last winter. And once they're listening, once they're following the story, then provided you're telling it right, they'll be wondering, 'What happens next?' And then, 'How does it end?' They're being drawn in by the natural power of storytelling. If things are going well, they're already thinking, 'What if we did this in our own context?'"

"This is how you persuade others to buy your idea? Through a story? Amazing!"

"You never persuade others to buy *your* idea. When it comes to something really important, to get any traction, it has to be *their own* idea. If you're trying to persuade them of *your* idea, you'll never succeed."

"How does it become their idea?" she asks.

"The trick is for the listeners to become their own storytellers. When that happens, it happens rapidly. You're talking about Timmy's winter in the Windy City, and they're sitting there thinking, 'We could do this! Why not?' The lis-

> The object of the storyteller is to enable the listeners to discover the truth for themselves.

teners are thinking through implementation even while you're still talking. By the time they leave the meeting, they already know what to do. With any luck they rush out and get into action."

"Isn't this a trick on the listeners? It's really my idea, and I'm tricking them into thinking it's their own idea?"

"Not really. It's up to the listeners whether to invent a new story for themselves. They're not being deceived. The story they tell themselves really is their own story, not your story. Each listener imagines a slightly different story, depending on her own situation."

"You mean each listener's story is different?"

"Precisely," I say. "The implications of the change idea for each listener will be different."

"But if each listener creates a different story, they'll be implementing different ideas. You know how Squirrel Inc. likes neatness and order."

Recognize that organizational storytelling is about telling authentic stories.

"Change is never orderly," I say. "A neat organization is already half dead."

"That may be, but Squirrel Inc. sure likes to see things tidy."

"I'm sorry, but the living part of the organization is untidy. It's a river of informal storytelling. It's flowing like white water. It's dynamic and full of life. If you want to interact with an organization, you have to get into that river. You've got to swim in it and with it."

She takes a long swallow. "You know it's terrible in a way."

"What is?"

"I come into a bar one day," she says, "and after that the whole world seems different. Now everywhere I look, I see stories. In the workplace. In meetings. In bars. At parties. Everywhere. It's pretty much all we do. Tell stories. Listen to stories. How come I never noticed this before?"

"You were taught to ignore it. So you ignored it."

"I need to rethink everything," she says. "My day. My job. My career. My life."

"For most individuals, it's a big shift," I say. "But hey! You're not the first one to make it. There are others in Squirrel Inc. who are using storytelling."

"What are they using it for?"

"To build community, transmit values, tame the grapevine, you name it."

"With the trouble Squirrel Inc. is in, I need to hear more."

"Why don't I invite them all to the bar here one night?"

"Who are they?" she says. "And how come I haven't heard about this before?"

I'm about to reply when one of my scruffier clients stumbles into the bar.

"Well, well, well," he says, without noticing that he's interrupting, "what have we here? Two conniving schemers! More trouble for Squirrel Inc.!"

"Hi, Mocha," I say. "What'll it be?"

"I can see it would be indiscreet of me to ask what you two are dreaming up?" Mocha continues. "No, don't tell me! Not another new strategy for Squirrel Inc.? First, we had nut burying, and then there was nut storing. Next what will it be? I've had it with zigs and zags! For heaven's sake, give us clarity! Clarity, clarity, clarity! You overpaid drones have so little to do, surely you could manage that?"

"The usual? Double ferment?"

"Exactly what I need to soothe and cool the ferment in my brain," says Mocha. "What a day I've had! So much commotion over what? Froth and bubble! Just when I thought I knew where Squirrel Inc. was heading, confusion makes his masterpiece. And now you two will double the trouble. Go ahead! Prove me wrong!"

"I'll do that," says Diana. "Give me a couple of days."

"You see what I mean," says Mocha. "A loyal employee of the great and noble firm of Squirrel Inc. has the temerity to petition for a smidgen of illumination from an illustrious champion of management, and what does he get? Subterfuge. Fog. Side-swerving deferral. You'll excuse me if I drink to your good health, my friends, while warning you that your nut-storing strategy doesn't have a hazelnut's chance in hell of being implemented."

"Why do you say that?" says Diana.

"The centurion guards!" says Mocha. "Watch out for the centurion guards! They protect and suckle the soul of the corporation to save it from basic change. A corporation, you see, is a very delicate mechanism. It doesn't suffer fundamental adjustment to its navigational system. Sure, you've made great presentations. Sure, you feel you're making gains. But wait till you're dealing with the managing committee. It'll be a different story. Trust me, I've seen it before. That's what the managing committee is for: to grind any bright new ideas into tiny, tiny pieces."

"We'll see about that," says Diana calmly.

"Believe me, it's been tried," says Mocha, passing his woodcup toward me for another extra-ferment. "Bold ideas. Brilliant thinking. Startling far-reaching plans, as full of promise as the bright summer sunshine, and then just when you're not expecting it, just when you're celebrating victory, they vote you off the island and you're doing the walk of shame. All that excitement and high flying comes to nothing!"

"Excuse me," says Diana abruptly. "You remind me—I have work to do."

"Good luck," I'm about to say, but she's gone before I can speak.

"Why did you do that?" I ask Mocha, passing him his extra-ferment.

"Introducing some reality into a conversation is always useful," he says, as the evening rush starts to come in all at once. Now I've no longer time for thought, let alone talk.

PERFORMING THE STORY
TO SPARK CHANGE
Guidelines

A story is always a selection of events from a wider universe of possibilities. In performing a springboard story, a leader has no need to acknowledge the selections, the exclusions, and the alternative points of view. These choices are made silently and out of the listeners' sight. Once made, the choices do not appear as choices at all. In performance, the story appears inevitable.

Some Suggestions for Performing the Story
- The leader immerses himself or herself in the world of the listeners—their language, habits, fears, and dreams.
- The leader makes the story fresh by reliving it as it is told.
- The leader focuses on perfecting a few stories that work well with a broad range of audiences, rather than trying to gather a large variety of stories.

- The leader enhances the storytelling performance through constant practice so that the story sounds like spontaneous conversation, as if an accomplished companion wanted to pass on something fresh and interesting that had just been thought of.
- The leader understands that there is a symmetry between storyteller and listeners, so even though the leader may have a wider experience than the listeners initially, the leader trusts the listeners to come to the same conclusion as the leader when given the same experience. The leader's purpose is to put the listeners in a position to achieve that parity. A leader tells the story so that the listeners discover the idea for themselves.[1]
- To get the listeners' attention before telling the story, the leader can frame the story, either by talking about the listeners' problems or by revealing a vulnerability.

A leader is not like a television cook showing others, step-by-step, how to make the perfect soufflé. The hard work of storytelling is performed invisibly. The leader is like the chef whose dishes are presented at the table: such a chef neither allows the diners to see the labor that went into a meal's creation nor expects them to share that labor. There are no salt and pepper shakers on the table.[2]

PART TWO

Narrative imagining—story—is the
fundamental instrument of thought.
Rational capacities depend upon it. It is our
chief means of looking into the future, of
predicting, of planning, and of explaining.

—MARK TURNER

Chapter Three

SAVE SQUIRREL INC. NIGHT

Seven Types of Organizational Storytelling

Storytelling is fundamental to the
human search for meaning.
—MARY CATHERINE BATESON

I'm often asked the name of my tavern. The truth is that it doesn't have one. In the twisted logic of squirrels—and in fact most living things—there's great cachet in anonymity, in smallness, in being hard to find. Squirrels think it's hip to be hanging out in a tiny space with no name.

This is a neighborhood place that comes into its own after dark, when the climbing woodbine exudes its curious perfume and there's no one about but bats and owls. I'm relieved the other birds are finally asleep. Not that I'm against birds. They mean well and they try to sound cheerful. I miss them in winter. It's not their fault that most of them have only one song. But sometimes their chirping gets on your nerves.

Tonight the idea is to have quiet. Some out-of-town Squirrel Inc. staffers have come into the city just for this. A few of them were already here last night, and things got rowdy. To tell you the truth, the tavern isn't large enough for what we have planned. I've stretched the seating capacity to the maximum. At least sixty squirrels are sitting on the birchwood benches and hanging from the branches. A large sign saying "Save Squirrel Inc." is also hanging from the branches.

I hear a brouhaha going on outside, and I look up from the apple daiquiris I'm whipping by hand. From all the clicking and clawing and gawking, it's someone who's attracting a lot of attention. When the crowd parts, it's Diana who's coming toward me.

Three weeks have gone by since this svelte exec from Squirrel Inc. was in here to get advice on using a story. Now here she is, all smoothly groomed, beaming and smiling, exuding success and potential celebrity.

"Welcome!" I say. "And congratulations!"

"Thanks to you!" she says with the widest of smiles.

"I gather you dazzled the managing committee."

"It was better than expected," she says.

"So we're celebrating your promotion?"

"Hang on," she says. "There's a catch."

"What's that?"

"Rumors of skullduggery," she whispers.

"What else is new? This is Squirrel Inc."

"Yes, but this is ominous," she says.

"Tell me more."

"It's the director of studies."

"Howe?"

"Exactly," she says. "He's up to something."

"What?"

"Not sure yet."

"We should find out," I say. "He's speaking here tonight."

"Howe?" she asks. "Here? Tonight?"

"He was invited," I say. "You're surprised?"

"Howe hates change," she says. "Any change. I wouldn't have expected him to be here."

"His talk is on sharing knowledge."

"If only he would do it, not just talk about it," she says, looking over the crowd. "Anyway, I don't see him."

"He said he'd be late. Important meeting."

"Not with the CEO?" she says with concern.

"He didn't say. Do you know the other speakers here tonight?"

She surveys the scene. "I know old Whyse, of course. And Sandra from the strategy group."

"You know Hester?" I ask. "She's into story as a tool to build community."

"Yes, I know Hester."

"And Mark? His specialty is values."

"I've heard of him. Very solid," she says. "And of course, Ted, the head of PR."

"He inquired," I say, "so I invited him."

"Fine," says Diana. "Squirrel Inc. could sure do with better press."

"And of course, Mocha, whom you met last time."

"Ah, yes, Mocha, the court jester."

"He's got more substance than one might suspect."

She watches my fellow bartender distribute drinks.

"They're impatient with the wait," I whisper. "I think we'll have to begin."

"Welcome!" I say to the assembled crowd. "Welcome to all my old friends in Squirrel Inc., and welcome to all the newcomers. As the regulars know, this isn't my bar. This is your bar—your home away from home, your place of respite, your friendly refuge from the hurly-burly of the workplace. I know what a dire crisis this is for Squirrel Inc. and how difficult this period is for each of you personally. I'm honored that you could find the time to be here tonight and explore how storytelling might help restore this firm to its former glory.

STORYTELLING CAN BE USED TO

- Spark action
- Communicate who you are
- Transmit values
- Get everyone working together
- Share knowledge
- Tame the grapevine
- Lead people into the future

"We're thrilled to have the most senior executives of Squirrel Inc. with us. First, the newest member of the managing committee: Diana."

At this point I'm interrupted by applause and a couple of cheers.

"As most of you probably know, she's just been tasked with transforming Squirrel Inc. into a nut-storing organization. For this task, she's being elevated to the position of vice president. Congratulations, Diana."

More loud applause.

"I've promised we'll show her the most important uses of storytelling as a leadership tool.

"We're also happy to welcome Ted, the director of PR at Squirrel Inc." Polite applause. "Splendid to have you with us, Ted.

"Finally, I'm delighted to announce that we'll shortly be joined by Howe, the distinguished director of studies at Squirrel Inc.

"So with these senior executives among us, I'm counting on you to deliver and show us what storytelling can do. Before we begin though, Diana will add a few words."

"Let me just say this," says Diana. "Squirrel Inc. is a wonderful company, but as we all know, it's seen better days. Once we were the corporate elite. Profits rose constantly. Our stock price was a high multiple of earnings. It's a glorious past, and we all want an equally beautiful future.

"Yet we're all conscious of the difficulty Squirrel Inc. is now in. Profits off. Market share eroding. We're all working day and night, but the results aren't coming. We know that change is inescapable, yet somehow we've been unable to get onto a different trajectory. Yet we also know that if we don't shift course, our very existence will be in question. If storytelling can help us, then I want to hear about it. So—let the show begin."

Amid the ensuing applause, Diana sits down next to Ted.

"Our first speaker tonight is Whyse," I say, as a scraggly looking animal makes his way to the center of the bar, amid solid applause.

"But, friends," I shout to the crowd, trying to make myself heard, "before we begin, let me remind you of the ground rules."

There is friendly booing and hooting.

"First of all, the good news. Drinks are on the house."

The hooting turns to cheers.

"But," I continue, "let's agree to keep the noise down."

Groans.

"The family of raccoons living lower down the tree was unhappy with what happened last night."

"Why don't we invite the raccoons?" says a squirrel sitting in front.

"You, Mocha, were one of the troublemakers," I say.

"The more the merrier!" says Mocha.

There are cries to begin.

"Over to you, Whyse," I say.

SEVEN TYPES OF ORGANIZATIONAL STORYTELLING
Guidelines

Once we glimpse the power of storytelling, we may imagine that we have stumbled upon a panacea—a universal solution. "Let's tell a story!" becomes the cry, often without any effort to understand what sort of story is needed for the organizational purpose at hand.

The reality is of course more complex. In storytelling, as in most fields, there is no single solution, no single silver bullet. Different forms of story are required to achieve different goals.

Seven Kinds of Stories

- A story to *ignite action*—a springboard story—is likely to require a true story with a positive tone, told in a minimalist fashion.
- A story to *share knowledge* is likely to be a true story with a negative tone, focused on a problem and presenting the context, the solution, and an explanation of the solution.
- A story to *get people working together* will be a moving story and will spark similar stories from the audience.
- A story to *lead people into the future* will be an evocative story, told with minimal detail.
- A story to *neutralize bad news* will be a true story that satirizes the bad news itself or the author of the bad news.
- A story to *communicate who you are* will tend to be a story in traditional form, with context, characters, and a plot.
- A story to *transmit values* will likely be a believable story describing how organizational leaders dealt with adversity.

Leaders who don't understand the different narrative patterns are likely to stumble into the wrong form of story. Having told the wrong form of story, they will then be disappointed when the intended effect fails to materialize, and they may blame the tool when the real reason for the failure lies in not understanding the array of storytelling patterns available and the different uses to which each can be put.

WHYSE'S STORY

How to Use Storytelling to Reveal
Who You Are and Build Trust

If you want to know me,
then you must know my story,
for my story defines who I am.

—DAN MCADAMS

hyse stands motionless until all the squirrels are quiet. Then he begins to talk. "If we're going save Squirrel Inc., we need to understand why it's in difficulty. Just now Diana mentioned declining profits and eroding market share. But these are just symptoms. At bottom the problem around here is that everything has turned impersonal. Remember when we all used to know who the CEO was? He built this company from nothing. He had character. He had values—a flesh-and-blood individual. But his successor? Who is he? You tell me. I hear his announcements. I listen to his decisions, but they change from day to day. Where does he really stand? To me he's still a blur. The result? Trust has plummeted. When you don't know who you're dealing with, everything becomes an issue.

"A traditional story communicates who you are. Needless to say, I forego the talk of new forms of stories. To me, a story is a story. Always has been. Always will be. Full of wonder and mystery. All this defining and categorizing of narratives, it's a waste of time. I say just tell the story. Let story do what story does best."

A traditional narrative has a beginning, a middle, and an ending. The beginning of the story sets the context of the narrative.[a]

"Whatever that is!" cries Mocha.

"Could you give us an example?" says Diana.

"Of course," says Whyse.

"This happened to me when I was very young. I was still living with my parents in an old mulberry tree. Our family had lived in it for generations. It had magnificent horizontal branches. I've always thought that mulberries are the best climbing trees. I had just learned how to run and jump from one branch to another. I was playing with my two brothers when suddenly my father came running toward us along the branch of an old tulip tree and told us to stop playing and follow him. And all three of us asked why.

The inciting incident of a narrative is the primary cause of all that follows.[b]

"*My father's face was grim and his whiskered lips were fixed and unsmiling. Then our mother joined us, and* she had the same pained look on her face. We followed them home, or at least what I'd thought of as home. Even before we arrived, I could hear the noise of machines and chain saws and earthmoving equipment. As we approached along a high branch of a pine tree, I could see humans walking around and mountains of earth being moved by bulldozers. The smell of gasoline fumes was terrible. But the worst was when we got closer and I looked for our home in the mulberry tree and I saw that the tree had been cut down, as had all the other trees nearby.

"We all stared at the devastation. The bulldozers kept moving more earth and the chain saws kept cutting down trees and then slicing the branches into pieces. I looked at the chopped-up mulberry tree and saw the luscious dark green leaves and the purple mulberries being trampled on and crushed by the muddy boots of the workmen, and I suddenly realized that I would never be nibbling those mulberries again.

The middle of a traditional narrative follows the progressive complications that flow from the inciting incident.

"'I wanted you to see this,' said my father. 'Squirrels must be watchful and prepared for the things that humans do.'

"It was a scene I'll never forget. But even more memorable was what happened after that. We were forced to move to a large park in the neighboring forest. As you could imagine, many families of squirrels were displaced. It was the beginning of winter, and all our food *supplies were cut off or destroyed by the construction work. It was hard to find a place to live because other families had taken the good trees.*

"So there were all these squirrels searching and scavenging and not really finding anywhere to live or enough to eat. With a cold winter coming on, things were beginning to look grim for us. Our mother told us not to worry, but I could see she was concerned.

"This went on for days, until one evening when all the squirrels who were using the park gathered together. It was a huge assembly, and a great debate took place.

The crisis or climax of a traditional narrative involves an action that resolves the forces that led to the progressive complications.

"The squirrels who had homes in the park spoke first. They talked about the problems that had been caused by the influx of new squirrels. How a family's acorns had been dug up and their whole store of food for the winter was gone. How even the nuts that were still on the trees were being eaten at a frightening rate by the new arrivals, so that the whole community would be in difficulty during the winter if the new squirrels were allowed to stay. Some squirrels said the newcomers should be forced to leave. But others said that wasn't fair because where would they go?

"Then one squirrel stood up and said that the problem was the humans. We should declare war on the humans since they were responsible for what had gone wrong.

"But someone said that would never work and everything would be infinitely worse than it was even now.

Why not join forces with humans and ask them to care for us and feed us?

"It was at this point that my father got up to speak. The last speech had made him angry. He was practically shouting when he made his opening declaration. 'Just remember one thing: they can cut down our mulberry tree, but they can't cut down our courage. We are squirrels!'

"He said that squirrels are independent. We live in the wild. It's a rough life, but it satisfies our basic nature. We can't live inside, sitting around waiting for human beings to feed us. We'd become not just tame but slaves. We'd be caricatures of squirrels.

"He ended as he began, 'That's why I say: they can cut down our mulberry tree, but they can't cut down our courage. We are squirrels!'

"And many in the audience said, 'Right!' Then others chipped in with tales of tough times in the past and how they had found a way to survive.

"And then someone asked what we were going to do. My father said that if we squabbled with each other and hid things, there was a risk that none of us would survive. But if we pooled our information about sources of food and kept everyone informed then there was a reasonable possibility that we would all live.

"When everyone wanted to know how this could be done, my father laid it all out and eventually everyone was satisfied that this was the way to go. And so we collaborated, and we did get through the winter. It was hard. It was cold. The winter was bitter. There were days when we were hungry. But whenever things were getting difficult, everyone would say, 'Remember the mulberry tree!' and we

would recall what squirrels are all about. Proud. Indepen-
dent. Ingenious. Wild. And so we survived.

"Now why am I telling you this story? Not just because it's a heartwarming story. I'm telling you this because it shows what sort of an individual my father was. That's what stories do for us.

A personal story can communicate who you are.

They're how we learn who we truly are."

As Whyse finishes, there's a storm of applause.

"That's powerful," says a voice from the crowd.

"But so slow," says Mocha. "It's as though you were talking to a herd of turtles. And anyway, what's it got to do with Squirrel Inc.?"

"It's central," says Whyse. "If our CEO could tell us his story, then we might understand what he's up to. When we don't have a clue who he is, everyone has questions. If we knew his story, we'd see who we're dealing with."

A resonant personal story may not need to have an explicit objective: the audience finds the meaning.

"Maybe I should explain the background," says Ted. "When the new CEO came on board, he faced a host of critical issues. Revenues were stagnating. Market share was eroding. Our stock price had tanked. His first instinct—and I think he was in the right on this—was to get a grip on the issues. So that's what he did. He met intensively with the executive team. Solving the problems of substance was more important than telling his own story. He had no wish to be just another celebrity CEO—all fur and no acorns."

"The problem is," says Whyse, "if we don't know who he is, how can any of us trust what he's doing on the substance? He comes across as impulsive, always changing his mind."

"I admit," says Ted, "we could have done a better job in getting his story out. Believe me, if you'd met him, you'd know what a wonderful individual he is. As you'll recall, when he arrived we distributed his curriculum vitae."

"That handout had the facts," says Whyse, "when what we needed was the narrative. How do the facts hang together? What are his passions? What is his background? For most of us in Squirrel Inc., he's still a cipher. He needs to speak to us from his heart."

> When you tell a story about someone else, it is also about you, as the storyteller.

"I'm not sure he'd be comfortable doing that," says Ted. "He'd prefer to stick with the issues."

"I'm not suggesting he forget the issues. But when he presents them, why not get him to tell his story? Perhaps some setback in his life and how he dealt with it? Something that reveals a vulnerability. Then we'd discover what made him the individual that he is. It would give depth to his presentation. We'd figure out what's making him tick."

"We have the corporate image to think of," says Ted. "Besides, he doesn't think his own story is particularly interesting."

"Then let him tell a story about someone else," says Whyse. "Someone he admires. Someone who had an influence on his life. Think about my mulberry tree story: it was a story about my father, but in the telling you learned about me."

"That's a thought," says Ted. "I could invite him to try that."

"When you tell a story," says Whyse, "you engage us in your experience. You entice us into your life. If we accept your invitation, we can get beyond mere facts or chatter. No matter what the story's about, we learn who you are. We begin to see things from your perspective. We begin to live your story. With luck, we begin to trust you. Your story becomes my story becomes our story. That's what we need from the CEO. We need to learn who on earth he really is."[1]

A story can also communicate a company's brand.[c]

Whyse returns to his place and there is more applause, then cries of "Next!"

"Whyse has a point," says Diana to Ted. "I think we ought to explore this."

Suddenly Whyse gets up again and says: "I've just remembered something else. I wanted to tell another sort of story too. This one isn't about me. This is about Squirrel Inc. and its brand. Just as a personal story can reveal who you are, so a company can present who it is by telling stories about itself."

"I need to hear more on that," says Diana.

"You will," I say, "but let's hear other speakers first."

"Then let me speak," says Hester, taking Whyse by the arm.

"Branding is key to our nut-storing strategy," says Diana to Ted.

Whyse gives way to Hester, who now takes the floor.

USING STORYTELLING TO REVEAL WHO YOU ARE AND BUILD TRUST
Guidelines

Communications in organizations are determinedly impersonal. Even the novice receptionist at the headquarters of a large organization quickly acquires the standard impersonal style of conversation. In times of rapid organizational change, a consequence is that trust plummets: people don't know whom they are dealing with.

"Stories of identity—narratives that help individuals think about who they are, where they come from, and where they are headed—constitute the single most powerful weapon in the leader's arsenal," Howard Gardner tells us. "The leader who can draw on or exploit the universal sensitivity to the classic story lines is the one who most often succeeds in convincing an audience of the merits of his or her program, policy or plan."[2]

Leaders use identity stories to describe their fundamental views about the world and explain how they developed these views. These are stories that communicate *"who I am."*[3]

Groups possess analogous *"who we are"* stories, which are less about the leader's personal experiences and attitudes and more about the joint experiences and attitudes of the people within the organization and their shared beliefs.[4]

Brands also embody stories of identity. A narrative that tells *"who the company is"* can tie the logo, the images, the products and services, the places, and the people of the organization together in a coherent whole.[5]

Stories of personal identity follow the lines of a traditional story. They talk about what happened to someone—the *hero or heroine*—who is usually also the storyteller. These stories have a *plot*. They are often told with *feeling*. Like tales for entertainment, these stories are typically colorful—*rich in context,* with an evocation of the sights and sounds and smells and tastes of the story's setting.

The aim of the identity story is to put a human face on the manager or the organization—and to show that the subject of the story has a heart.

Chapter Five

HESTER'S STORY

How to Use Storytelling to Get Individuals to Work Together

Competition intensifies. . . . Change is constant.
Customers take charge. . . .
We need something entirely different.

—MICHAEL HAMMER AND JAMES CHAMPY

Hester comes to the front. Gradually the noise subsides until there is total silence. She begins talking very quietly:

> *"What Whyse says is fine as far as it goes, but right now the biggest issue for Squirrel Inc. is getting everyone to work together. Everyone says it's essential. Yet once our business ran into difficulty, collaboration collapsed. Managers distanced themselves from company decisions. Each unit focused more and more on its own issues. As revenues declined, everyone pointed the finger at someone else. Problem solving gave way to self-protection. The game was blame others before they blame you. Everyone fought to*

*keep a share of the shrinking budget. Since the news was
generally negative, internal communications dried up.
No one was actively hiding anything—there was just no
reason to meet. We all knew steadily less and less about
what was going on in other parts of the company. Everyone talked about collaboration, but in practice it didn't
happen.[1]*

    *"Then, suddenly, one day there it was in my divi-
sion. I was home. There was no need for more searching.
What I had been yearning for turned out to be so easy and
obvious. Sometimes I ask myself in retrospect, How could I
have missed something so simple?*

    *"Whyse said his story revealed who he was. But I
believe storytelling has another meaning completely. It's
not just about understanding. It has to do with action. It
can lead to everyone working together. Imagine if we could
make that happen throughout Squirrel Inc."*

Hester pauses as if in thought, then continues.

*"We all want to be part of a larger story. We want a larger
story that's shared. We've become too individualistic at
Squirrel Inc. Community is what's missing. It's something
we once had. Somehow we lost it. Now we can restore it,
with a story.*

    *"Think about the mulberry tree story. Everyone
who was living in the park that winter felt a sense of community. Each saw that survival depended on the group.
Helping others wasn't a duty offered begrudgingly. It was
genuine caring. There was interdependence, both among
individuals and within the whole community.*

    *"What happened was astonishing. It wasn't
planned. It happened naturally and organically. No one*

foresaw it or even recognized it when it began. Everyone saw the benefits of collective effort. It was more than just the success of getting through the winter. The individuals came to value the solidarity that the community represented.

"I heard about what happened there. The next year the situation had changed. There was no need for any special measures to get through the winter. But the arrangements that had been put in place were maintained. When new squirrels were born, it was a cause for general rejoicing. When a squirrel died, the families felt responsible for the next of kin. Some of the squirrels had opportunities and could have gone somewhere else. But most of them opted to stay. They preferred to endure the ups and downs of their community. It was theirs. They found it rewarding. For them, continuing allegiance to the community, and to its way of life, became an end in itself."[2]

A rough definition of a group is a set of individuals who share the same stories and see the same meaning in them.

"Splendid!" says Mocha. "But tell me, what's the connection with Squirrel Inc.?"

"The connection is this," says Hester very quietly. "We used the same process of sharing stories to generate a community within our division."

"In Squirrel Inc.?" asks Ted.

"Yes," says Hester. "What we saw is that when individuals have shared stories, they work together much better. That's virtually a definition of a group or a community: it's a set of individuals who know the same stories and see the same meaning in them. So when we accelerated the sharing of stories, collaboration took off."

"How did it happen?" Diana asks.

Hester says:

STEP ONE

Bring the group together physically.

"The first step was for all of us to get together, face to face. We were used to seeing each other around. But that wasn't enough. Each of us had to meet with all the others. We were individuals who in the normal course of work didn't talk to each other much. Some of us had radically different backgrounds. On the surface, we had very little in common. The first step was to get together."

"I've always said face-to-face is best," says Whyse.

Hester continues:

STEP TWO

Establish an open agenda.

"The second step was to use an open agenda. For our manager this was the most terrifying element. At first, he found it difficult to envisage a meeting that began with no set agenda. He'd been raised on a diet of directing and deciding. The open-agenda meeting was an affront to this kind of thinking. And yet, to create a safe space, he eventually saw that he had to set goals aside for the moment. Goals had to grow organically. Then the group itself discovered and determined its own identity."

"That's what management so often tries to eliminate," says Whyse.

"The third step was to spark a process of collective story-telling. We had someone tell a story that resonated with everyone present. It was the story of a staff member who'd tackled a difficult issue. It moved all of us as individuals. We discovered something we had in common.

STEP THREE
Start with a moving story.

"It was like when Whyse told us his story tonight: you saw how a special feeling came over us. Our hearts went out to the families that were displaced. We relived their experience. It was as if we'd become part of their community. Well, the same thing happened in our division. We relived that staff member's experience."

"And then what?" asks Diana.

"And then the fourth step was for all of us in the division to share our stories. That happened very naturally. The first story led to another. Listeners felt like offering something in return. Our feelings were 'I've got a story to tell like that' and 'I'd like to hear more stories like that.' It was a chain reaction.

STEP FOUR
Create a process of sharing meaningful stories among the members of the group.

The two interests together generated the energy. It became almost a competition to see who could tell the best story.

Once we'd done this, it helped everyone see meaning in what we were doing and why we were doing it. Instead of a hostile, threatening place, the workplace started to feel like home."[3]

"And the outcome?" Diana asks.

"It was startling to see how fast we all fused into a community. Energy was generated. If there'd been no outlet for all that energy, it would have been a huge letdown. Happily, our manager had an action plan. He was ready for success. He supported the community that emerged. And things just went on from there. After that, the bickering and the finger pointing disappeared. Previously intractable problems became manageable. We had a whole new level of effectiveness."

STEP FIVE
Have an action
plan ready.

"Could we use this for introducing the nut-storing strategy?" says Diana.

"Why not?" says Hester.

"I've been to those team-building retreats," says Mocha. "New bowl, same soup."

"No, Mocha, this is different," says Hester. "This wasn't one of those tawdry team-building days where no one levels and everyone goes right back to the same old ways regardless. Through the storytelling, individuals invited colleagues into their lives, so that others could understand how they felt and vice versa. And the storytelling was mutual. Once the floodgates of communication were open, our whole division functioned differently. The storytelling responded to what individuals in the division wanted, but it also met Squirrel Inc.'s needs. We weren't trying to turn the whole of Squirrel Inc. into a community. We built a community *within* Squirrel Inc."

"In any event, we should spread the news to the rest of the company," says Ted.

"This will be important for nut storing," says Diana with energy. "We bring everyone together so that each can see how to contribute. But I see Mocha doesn't agree."

"I think it's brilliant," says Mocha. "My issue is, can we count on Squirrel Inc.? This firm isn't a community. I wonder if it will ever be. You can grow a community in your division. Fine! Your community nurtures you. Perfect! But since when has Squirrel Inc. been willing to make this kind of commitment? Suppose management cuts your budget or even eliminates your division. Will the feeling of community survive that?"

> Companies are not themselves communities, but they can do things that foster community.

"It's possible," says Hester. "It depends on the community spirit. And I agree; it won't be easy. If hierarchy invades the communities, they can die. Equally, if the communities try to take on the management, they can perish in the attempt. The communities and the management have to learn to live together. Their mutual future depends on it. It's in these communities and informal groupings that anything innovative or creative will occur. They'll drive the growth of Squirrel Inc. They'll build customer loyalty. If the staff just march in lockstep to orders, Squirrel Inc. will wither and die. We're talking about a new metaphor for the organization in a world of rapid flux. Storytelling is at the core."

There's applause from the audience, and Hester returns to her place.

"Community is fine," says Mark, "but community depends on values."

"OK, Mark," I say, "you're on."

USING STORYTELLING TO GET INDIVIDUALS TO WORK TOGETHER
Guidelines

Every management textbook ever written has insisted on the centrality of getting people to work together. Yet when one tries to find where the textbook spells out how to make that happen, typically the information is missing or so sketchy as to be unhelpful. "Create cross-functional commit- tees" and "stimulate new conversations" are typical sugges- tions. What will those committees talk about? What will be the content of those conversations? When an organization is in a downward spiral of secrecy, denial, finger pointing, and turf protection, the risk is that the new committees and con- versations will simply perpetuate the negativity.

A leader builds a community by generating a shared narrative around common concerns and goals. The initial narrative must be sufficiently moving that all parties share the same meaning from the story and see it as an entice- ment to hear more. The listeners' reactions ought to be, "I know a story like this that I'd like to share," and, "I'd like to hear more stories like that." One story sparks another. And another. If the process continues, those involved are no longer merely a collection of disparate individuals. Through the use of the narrative imagination, they have a shared perspective. A process of sharing narratives enables community to emerge naturally.

Steps for Accelerating the Formation of a Community
- The leader brings the participants together.[4]
- The leader establishes an open agenda.
- The leader tells or sparks a moving story.
- The leader encourages a process of sharing stories among the group.
- The leader has an action plan ready to capitalize on the energy generated.

This approach is applicable not only to team building but also to knowledge sharing,[5] mergers and acquisitions,[6] and supply chain management.[7]

Caveat: hierarchy provides structure and discipline. Community generates collaboration and innovation. A leader recognizes that community and structure are in constant tension but mutually dependent on each other for ultimate survival.

Chapter Six

MARK'S STORY

How to Use Storytelling to Transmit Values

As its campfires glow against the dark, every culture
tells stories to itself about how the gods lit up the
morning sky and set the wheel of being in motion.

—DAVID BERLINSKI

"There's something even more fundamental at stake in
Squirrel Inc.," says Mark. "Trust and community are
wonderful, but they can't happen without a sense of shared
values. We had this sense once in Squirrel Inc., but we lost it.
If we're going to save Squirrel Inc., we have to get it back."

"I agree," says Ted. "And the CEO also believes
it's key."

"And he's right," says Mark. "It's vital to our survival.
One piece of creative accounting, and this firm could be on
its knees. If some branch manager does a dirty deal, we're out
of business. Squirrel Inc.'s very existence depends on everyone

having the right values. While revenues are declining, the risk of someone doing something stupid gets bigger every day."

"It's a risk, yes," says Ted. "That's why the CEO has already done so much."

"Ted, I'm sorry to have to say this," says Mark, "but putting up posters and circulating cards with lists of values, as the CEO is now doing—this ain't going to work! Values don't come from cards or posters. They reside in the stories that are told and acted on and our reaction to those actions. When something dramatic happens that demonstrates our values, it becomes a story that gets told and retold. Our imaginations continue to give it fresh resonance. That's what we used to have with the old CEO."

Values are established by actions of the leaders and are transmitted by narratives that exemplify them.

"I knew him too," says Whyse. "He was like a rock."

"That was before my time," says Hester.

Mark says:

"He was passionate about telling the truth and getting the whole story out. He knew there was no point in hiding bad news. He was always the first to get it out in the sunlight. If you'd ever met him, you'd know what I mean.

"When he reviewed the accounts, he made sure they used plain language that made clear what was involved. There were no hidden costs off the books. No secret payoffs for the executive team. No hanky-panky. No hocus-pocus. He ran an open house.

"When he said something, he meant it. He maintained it was a matter of good faith to live by the let-

ter of our agreements as well as the intent. I can still recall the way he looked at me when I heard him say that for the first time. You knew that you could count on that value. He lived by it. And he expected us to live by it as well.

"I remember when he learned that a hard-working subordinate had lied on his job application about something he said he'd done. Instead of firing him, he took the employee aside and asked, 'What is it going to take for you to make good on what you said you'd done?' He believed in doing the right thing. He felt being a leader meant being true to yourself and to your employees.[1]

To transmit values, use stories about how the leaders dealt with adversity.

"Stories like that one helped establish our values. When the stories circulated, everyone absorbed the values and understood how things were done around here.

"All of us at Squirrel Inc. heard and lived those stories for years. We weren't just doing whatever was necessary for Squirrel Inc. to make money. We were also committed to telling the truth and sticking to our word. So long as we were clear that this was the story we were living, and Squirrel Inc. was clear on it too, there wasn't any problem."

"Our founder was legendary," says Ted. "He still gets us tremendous press."

"And his successor?" says Whyse.

"The same," says Ted. "When you're the CEO of a company, you're the steward of a lot of individuals, including

71

the employees, shareholders, and customers. If the steward-ship attitude isn't there, if you're in it just to make money, all bets are off. Fortunately I can assure you our new CEO has the same passion for integrity as for enhancing shareholder value."

To transmit values, leaders need to live their stories as well as tell them.

"Try telling that to the investors if he doesn't hit his numbers," says Mocha.

"We're going to do both," says Ted. "We'll hit our numbers and we'll stick to our values. What I don't see is how a mere story can generate values. Values are things like honesty or integrity. You can tell a story to illustrate them, but the values are separate from the narrative. Aren't you confusing the two?"

"Let me explain it this way," says Mark. "When you look at abstractions like honesty or integrity on a poster, they become mere artifacts. Things hanging on the wall. Narra-tives are active and dynamic. You live the story as well as tell it. The story becomes part of you."

To transmit values use stories that are like parables: believable and generally positive in orientation.

"Can you give us an exam-ple?" says Sandra.

"It's like that story about the squirrel who told a lie on his recruitment application," says Mark. "In one sense, what hap-pened is dismal: a squirrel lied. Yet the CEO found a way to turn a negative into a positive. He converted it into a story of possibility, the possibility of becoming authentic, of becom-ing honestly who you say you are. As that story got told and retold, it communicated his values and in fact embodied them. The narrative is more important than any abstract tag you put on it. Once people heard the story, they grasped what it meant, because they'd followed the story."

"Surely there'd be more clarity if you spelled out the values," says Ted.

To transmit values, focus on telling the story rather than listing abstract values.

"People remember stories," says Mark. "They don't recall abstractions. I won't embarrass everyone by asking now how many here tonight can recite the official values of Squirrel Inc. When you think about values as abstractions, they become lifeless objects. When values are transmitted through a narrative, we understand what they meant in that time and place, and we can figure out how they apply in our own lives. Living values are active—they're an ongoing conversation between realities of the past and the possibilities for the future. If you print them on posters or cards, they sound unnatural and fabricated: that's when they're likely to die."

To transmit values, focus on stories with meaning for the here and now.

"So the story of that employee communicated the values as well as embodying them," says Diana.

"Exactly," says Mark. "It was a narrative that communicated what it meant for someone to work in Squirrel Inc. As that narrative was told and retold, it had implications for how we would live in future. It was by sharing and living such narratives that our values were established."

"Could I ask a question?" says Diana.

"Fire away," I say.

"What do you do when you don't agree with the orders that come down the line? What do you do when the top insists that you implement decisions and you have a different view?"

"In a conflict," says Mark, "you have to balance contending values—in this case honesty to yourself and loyalty to the organization. If you do that openly, then later on, when you have a real emergency, everyone is more likely to believe what you say."[2]

In a difficult issue, contending values have to be balanced.

"Maybe it would be useful to have rules for these things," says Hester.

"Not necessarily," says Mark. "Rules are shorthand versions of values. They can be useful guides for simple issues. 'Tell the truth.' 'Keep your promises.' But they don't help you when you get to a difficult issue, like a conflict between telling the truth and being loyal to the firm. Here you have competing values, each legitimate in its own way. The rules don't solve the problem. Sorting it out means deciding what kind of individual you are. It means choosing the story of which you want to be a part. Rules are not the end of knowledge: they're the beginning."

It's now getting so loud in the tavern, it's all but out of hand; once a party starts, it's not easy to stop it, even if you want to.

"Look!" Diana whispers to me, nodding toward a tall tawny squirrel, stalking into the bar. "Here comes the cool of the evening."

A sudden hush comes over the crowd.

"My name is Howe," he announces loudly. "I was invited to speak tonight on stories that share knowledge: am I in the right place?"

"You certainly are," I say, coming forward to greet him. "Thanks for coming. You're talking after our next speaker, Mocha."

"I'm very pressed for time," says Howe. "I'd like to speak right away if you don't mind."

"Well, Mocha was meant to speak next," I say, "but I'm sure he'll yield the floor."

Then, just as I'm about to introduce Howe, Mocha suddenly cuts in and says, "Now my time has finally come, why should I step aside?" He emits a noise somewhere between a hiccup and a burp, which sparks laughter all around.

> Rules are the beginning of establishing a sense of values, not the end.

The audience begins to chant, "Mocha! Mocha!"

"Do you mind if I wet my whistle?" says Mocha, looking around for his woodcup.

"Enough is enough," I say.

"Enough?" says Mocha. "'Enough' is a complex concept. May I explain the main points?"

"That won't be necessary," I say.

"Then why did you mention it?" says Mocha. "I drink when I have occasion and also when I have no occasion. So listen to what I say and draw your own confusions."

"It will just be a few minutes," I assure Howe and invite him to take his place.

"As I say, I don't have much time," says Howe testily.
"Mocha won't be long," I say. "Will you, Mocha?"
"He's already said enough," says Howe.
"You're on, Mocha," I say. "And be prompt."

USING STORYTELLING TO TRANSMIT VALUES
Guidelines

How can a leader instill the values in an organization that will make controls almost unnecessary? This isn't about cleaning up a mess that has already happened. It's about continuously anticipating future problems that could permanently impair the earning power of the core business. How can this be accomplished when the firm is operating in environments where integrity isn't central or in situations where there is a track record of scandal?

Organizational leaders can learn a lesson from the great religious teachers—they all used *parables* to transmit values. Parables are stories that are believable and that have a limited amount of context, a positive orientation, and an obvious moral.[3]

Points for Crafting a Story to Transmit Values
- The leader establishes values through actions, particularly actions that deal with adversity.
- Values are transmitted by stories about the actions that have established the values.

- These stories have meaning in the here and now: they are not merely lists of abstract values.
- In dealing with difficult issues, the leader recognizes the need to balance contending values.
- The leader recognizes that rules are the beginning of developing values, not the end.

Caveat: actions speak louder than words. It's not enough for the story to be told. Leaders have to live the values consistently.

Chapter Seven

MOCHA'S STORY

How to Use Storytelling to Tame the Grapevine

> Though this be madness,
> yet there is method in't.
> —WILLIAM SHAKESPEARE

"**M**y fellow squirrels," says Mocha. "Tonight we've heard that stories inspire individuals, reveal identity, build community, and transmit values. Fine! But we won't save Squirrel Inc. unless we stop the rumors that are flying and put brakes on the bad news. This is a whole different pile of nuts."

"For example?" says Sandra.

"We've all heard the talk about Squirrel Inc. being taken over by our chief rival," says Mocha. "The CEO has denied it. Ted's issued circulars confirming it's untrue. But the rumor keeps growing. Now it's almost the sole focus of conversation throughout the company. Staff spend their time positioning themselves for the transition."

"That's so," says Ted. "But we've already denied the rumor. What else can we do?"

"You can't argue with a rumor," says Mocha. "You satirize it! How could we be taken over by a company whose financial condition is even more critical than Squirrel Inc.'s? Ridiculous! Tying two stones together won't make them float. A satire disarms an argument by letting us view its subterfuges."

"You know," volunteers Ted, "as director of PR at Squirrel Inc., I find this intriguing. Coping with rumors and bad news is a huge part of what I have to do. At the upper levels of management, the world may seem serene, but lower down, the rumor mill is going full tilt."

"Ted, you're not taking this buffoon seriously?" asks Howe.

"Personally, Howe, I'd like to hear what he has to say," says Ted.

"Thank you, I appreciate that," says Mocha. "My fellow squirrels, as Ted points out, the rumor mill doesn't stop just because Howe gives it an instruction. Squirrel Inc. may be able to terminate an employee, but it can't terminate the grapevine. Of all corporate citizens, this is the most insidious."

"I agree," says Ted. "This is a real problem for us right now. But what can we do?"

"We're dealing here with the shadow side of the organization. It's hidden, but pulsing, throbbing, moving, and full of life. It's where deals are cut, where reputations are ruined, where policies are dropped, where the guilty are promoted, where the innocent are convicted, and where the undiscussable is discussed. Once we realize that it's there, we can harness that energy and use it to defuse the bad news."

"Why should the news be bad?" asks Howe. "We may be going through a rough patch, but this is still a well-run company."

"I'm sorry to say," says Mocha, "that the dirt has been earned. Managers have become figures of fun. Teamwork? What a scream! Coffee with the boss? Give me a break! I mean, a real break. When the grand maharajas of management get up to speak, is anyone listening? When we hear the gurgle from the gutter known as the HR department, how many are paying attention? When the lizards from accounts run us through their numbers, is anyone focusing?

"Managers like Howe can't even imagine this much bad news. And even if they can, what are their options? The trick is to work *with* the flow not *against* it. You use the energy of the network to circulate an alternative version. You ridicule the bad news into oblivion. Humor becomes a tool, a kind of virus, that drives the bad stuff out."

Jettison the mushroom culture: tell it like it is.

"But how?" asks Ted.

Mocha says:

"The first step in taming the grapevine is a commitment to tell the truth. Tell it like it is and let the chips fall where they may. You have to dump the mushroom culture. You know: keeping everyone in the dark and feeding them manure. You have to level with everyone—all the news, all the time."

"You said to use humor," says Ted, "but this doesn't sound funny."

"Patience, my friend," says Mocha.

"The second step in taming the grapevine is to parody the bad news. Let's suppose there's a rumor afoot that management is on the verge of launching another major reorganization."

"Oh no," whispers Diana to Ted. "Not another one?"

"If you deny it, you're done for. If you ignore it, it gets bigger. If you ask how it got started, that ensures its spread. So what can you do? Well, if the bad news isn't true, then you can show that it's so ridiculous it can't be true. When you give a humorous view of the bad news, you stop being a victim. You show that you have the bad news within your grip. You adopt the posture of the gods. You invite life in with a smile."

A satire can find humor in the bad news itself.

"But what if the bad news is true?" asks Ted.

"If the bad news is true, there's nothing a satire can do. If the accounts department really is run by lizards, then no joke can save you. You'd better admit the truth and fix any resulting problem. If the management really is planning yet another reorganization, you may as well say so. But if it isn't true, a parody can show why the rumor is unreasonable or incredible or both."

"The gossip about takeovers and reorganizations is nonsense," says Ted. "But when the bad news is true, and goodness knows, we've had plenty of that recently, we've had the CEO get out there and talk about it and set it in a broader context. Even if nothing can be done about it, he's helped everyone get a sense of the bigger picture. He's spelled out what caused the bad events to happen and why. I believe that's what leadership is about: setting events in perspective."

"That's fine," says Mocha, "so long as you stick to the truth and provided you have some credibility. But if the bad news isn't true, and you try simply to deny it, then all hell breaks loose. Merely denying the rumor is futile. So hit it with some wit. Parody the bad news until it shrivels into insignificance."

"When you're parodying something" says Howe, "it distracts you from serious action."

"It's through humor that we see the truth, particularly the truth that others don't want us to see," says Mocha.

A satire is generally ineffective against a rumor that is true.

"The truth?" says Howe. "You, Mocha, use humor to put others down."

"Only those who deserve to be put down," says Mocha. "When you can laugh at something, it means that you've mastered it. When you're crying and whining, that means it's mastered you."

"Your problem, my friend, is that you've been mastered by drink," says Howe.

"I agree," says Mocha with a hiccup. "I serve many masters, and none more devotedly than my drink. Which reminds me, where's my woodcup?"

"Are you done yet?" asks Howe.

Mocha says:

"The third step in taming the grapevine is to find humor in whoever launched the bad news. Again it's the truth-telling element that has the effect. So if I were to call my friend here, my very good friend Howe, an odious rodent, you might giggle for an instant. But it wouldn't affect your view of what he says, because there's no truth to the humor. It's just the hard edge of laughter without any heart. Humor without heart becomes mere abuse or sneering. Genuine humor is a blend of love and truth. But if I were to call Howe a nitpicking pedant of a professor, you might smile, and this time there's more: the truth of the description gets under his skin and reminds him to be less uptight."

"Do we have to listen to this?" says Howe stiffly.

"I suspect you've hurt his feelings," says Sandra.

"That is, if he has any," says Mocha. "It's a risk. Wit is tricky. It singles out an individual and picks on the weakest point. If there's a grain of truth to the humor, it's a truth that can wound. Even if the intent is friendly, the hurt can be enduring. True humor comes with truth but combines it with a smile. We sidestep the vicious and the cynical. We delight in life like a child.

"True humor provides perspective. It lifts up the downtrodden. We see that in the vast scheme of things our difficulties are hardly worth crying about. At the same time it cuts the powerful down to size. It zooms in on all those who presume themselves to be better than they are."

"Your insults don't affect me in the slightest," says Howe.

"Maybe Howe is insensitive as well as a pedant," says Mocha. "But others are less so. For instance, if I were to suggest that our esteemed bartender here is suffering from a broken heart, some of you might see his viewpoint."

"Enough of that," I say.

"If I were to suggest," says Mocha, "that Diana here, the rising star of Squirrel Inc. who is gracing us with her presence here tonight, is—"

"Have you finished, Mocha?" I say, interrupting his tirade.

"Not by a long shot," says Mocha.

"The fourth step in taming the grapevine is to find humor in yourself. As you see, you can get into trouble by making fun of others. It's safer to make fun of something closer to home—yourself. Someone with vulnerabilities can't be all bad. On the surface the joke is about you, but it also satirizes others. By laughing at yourself, you may get the grapevine to give you a break."

Humor can take the form of satirizing your own thoughts or actions.

"Can you give us an example?" asks Ted.

"I wouldn't know how. Listening to all you folks who are so much cleverer than I am, with this enormous respect for Squirrel Inc. that's almost awe. Even love. Well, congratulations! I'm happy for you all. It's a wonderful company, yes. But love? I'm sorry. That's something I haven't been able to manage.

*"Lord knows, I've done my utmost. I've been to
the retreats. I've had coffee with my boss. I've worked on
my performance flaws. I've developed my growth goals. I've
honed my teamwork skills. Yes, I've done all that, but at
the end of the day, if you ask me to love Squirrel Inc., I
just can't manage it."*

"This isn't serious," says Howe.

"Why should I be serious," says Mocha, "when wit
trumps every other card in the pack? Despite what my friend,
the professor here, might tell you, humor is a higher form of
thought than either analysis or tragedy. The professor fears not
being taken seriously, as if being serious means you exude the
truth. Typically it's the opposite. Being serious means some
kind of con is going on. That's why seriousness is tiring.

"It's only when we're laughing that we see the world
in its flowing holistic beauty. Humor sparks renewal. When
we laugh, we become one with the universal flux. That's why
humorists are the accredited representatives of the future.
They lead from wherever they are, because wit is irresistible.
It's a universal solvent, dissolving every position, privilege, and
prohibition. When we turn life into a carnival, we're both
actors and audience. It's not just something to be witnessed.
It's something that we live. It's a universal spirit. It's vivid for
all participants."

At this point, Mocha performs a mock-serious bow as
if he had just given a concert. In the midst of the mixed
applause, I apologize to Howe for Mocha's performance. If
we don't take care, the raccoons will be back.

Ted turns to Diana and says, "It seems a little off-beat
for the CEO."

"What's the option?" says Diana. "If he doesn't do something, the rumor mill will kill him."

"How about an encore?" says Mocha.

"Thanks, but you're finished," I say.

Getting back to business, I call on Howe. "Go ahead, sir, you're on."

"I'm sorry to spoil the party," says Howe with a sigh, "but I have bad news for the Mochas of this world. Despite what we've just heard, the meaning of life doesn't lie in one-liners. We won't solve Squirrel Inc.'s problems with tomfoolery. To be sure, I could amuse you with gags till you rolled on the ground and the tears flowed down your cheeks."

"Why don't you try us!" cries Mocha, downing another extra-ferment.

USING STORYTELLING
TO TAME THE GRAPEVINE
Guidelines

Every organization has a shadow aspect, hidden but alive—pulsing, throbbing, and moving. Once a leader realizes its existence and its role in the organization, its energy can be harnessed to deal with the rumors and bad news that flow through it.

If the bad news or rumor is untrue or unreasonable, it may be possible to tell a story that attaches to the bad news and sends it to oblivion.

A story to tame the grapevine provides a striking insight, often using *humor or incongruity* as its mechanism. It draws attention to some inconsistency in *the bad news* and invites the reader to conclude, "This news is unreasonable! It couldn't be true! How ridiculous for me to have taken this seriously!" The story usually satirizes the bad news or the author of the bad news or the storyteller himself.

Most jokes are not satiric. Rather they play on the existing views and prejudices of the listeners, leaving those perspectives untouched. A satire aims at *subverting the listeners' beliefs,* perhaps permanently.

Although stories to tame the grapevine are usually remarkably *brief,* they are tricky to construct. However, they are immensely powerful when they are successful. Such stories typically *seize on some hidden or unexpected aspect of the bad news* and point out its incongruity.

Caveat: humor is a dangerous tool.[1] Humor without heart becomes mere abuse or sneering, which will generate a well-deserved backlash. Finely tuned satire is *a blend of love and truth.* It is a festive laughter. It is not merely putting someone down in an isolated comic event. It is directed at all and everyone, including the storyteller. The entire world is seen in its droll aspect. This laughter is ambivalent: it is gay and triumphant and at the same time mocking and deriding. It asserts and denies. It wounds and heals. It's a universal solvent, dissolving privilege and prohibition.[2]

Chapter Eight

HOWE'S STORY

How to Use Storytelling
to Share Knowledge

Scientific knowledge, like all human knowledge,
consists primarily of explanations.
—DAVID DEUTSCH

"**A**ll this talk," says Howe, "is beside the point. The way to save Squirrel Inc. is to keep a steady focus on our goal and use knowledge in support of that goal. All the world knows that knowledge triggers efficiency. Knowledge generates effectiveness. Knowledge ignites innovation. Knowledge gets things done. More important than money, more brilliant than light, knowledge is the blood, the pulse, the spark, the flame of the economy.

"Look closely at anything going forward and you'll observe knowledge at work. Examine anything in trouble and you'll discover a problem with knowledge. Of course I'm talking now about genuine knowledge, not conjecture or opinion or impressions. I mean knowledge backed by hard evidence and studies and numbers and results. Because the currency is knowledge, the highest-value narratives are those that transmit understanding. This isn't about folk tales or jokes. I'm talking plain, practical bottom-line value. I'm talking about the kind of knowledge that made Squirrel Inc. great."

Unlike most other stories, a knowledge-sharing story doesn't need a hero or heroine.

The crowd is now silent.

"The knowledge-sharing story is about finding the solution to a problem by way of an explanation. It's quite different from a story about heroes and heroines and their triumphs and tragedies. A knowledge-sharing story tells of the pursuit of the truth. It's wrestling with problems and securing their solutions. It's the excitement of science. It's the delight of finding things out."

"Perhaps you mean that the problem is your villain," says Sandra, "and your hero is the solution."

"No," says Howe. "It's a different kind of story. Let me give you an example.

A knowledge-sharing story has four elements: problem, setting, solution, and explanation.

"There was once a chicken being kept by a farmer and fed each day with plentiful corn. The chicken's problem was why was she being fed so well? She watched the farmer as he prepared her food each day. He observed her eating it. He seemed interested in her well-being. He seemed pleased that she was growing fat and sleek. She thought about it and came up with a logical explanation: 'The farmer wants me to be happy.' After that, her solution

to her problem was simply to relax and enjoy her existence, content in knowing that she would continue to be fed by the farmer. But then one day the farmer came, and instead of feeding her, he strangled her to death and cooked and ate her."

"The poor bird!" says Mocha.

Howe continues:

"The chicken had missed something. If she'd paid more attention to the setting, she might have noticed that her fellow chickens were disappearing one by one. This attention to detail would have led her to a second possible explanation, namely, that the farmer was fattening her for his own eating pleasure. Instead the chicken believed her explanation of the benevolent farmer. So she never got to genuine knowledge. By the time the truth emerged, she was dead.[1]

A knowledge-sharing story describes the setting in enough detail that the solution is linked to the problem by the best available explanation.

"Whatever we observe in the world has multiple explanations. In telling a knowledge-sharing story that shows the solution to a problem, we must describe enough of the setting and the explanation so that we can apply the solution to a similar problem in a different situation."

"Maybe the chicken wasn't really interested in understanding why the farmer was feeding her?" says Mark.

"That's the point," says Howe. "A key to acquiring real knowledge involves deciding to find out. When we have an interesting experience, we must develop a hypothesis and explore where it might lead."

"What if we choose the wrong hypothesis?" says Sandra.

In a knowledge-sharing story, it's important to define your knowledge-sharing goal.

"We admit the mistake," says Howe, "and choose another possible explanation."

"But if you decide in advance what you want to know," says Ted, "how can you ever innovate? Squirrel Inc. needs new ideas, not just confirmation of what we already know."

"Starting in one area doesn't mean you won't find out other things," says Howe.

"Let me cite an example from one of our recent studies. We were conducting research to determine the extent of the market for a possible new business in nut storing. In the process of conducting that study, what did we find? Lo and behold, we stumbled on the fact that there are still large, unexploited pockets of market for our existing business of nut burying. Whole groups of customers that we hadn't thought of had unmet needs that

Allow for serendipity; it can reveal unexpected insights.

we could easily exploit without a costly change to our existing strategy. That's not what we set out to find, but it was a very significant discovery.

"Knowledge, my friends, is infinite. The whole universe can be detected in a single hickory nut if you study it enough. So if you try to understand everything, you end up understanding nothing. You have to decide what you're trying to find out. You set out with a hypothesis, but you don't stick to it blindly. Thanks to serendipity, you might learn something else along the way. But you keep your eye on where you're heading. Otherwise you get lost."

"Sounds like hard work," says Whyse.

"Precisely," says Howe. "Acquiring knowledge *is* hard work. You have to do the patient, painstaking work of sifting through the evidence. You have to check and verify the explanation to see whether it's the best. You earn knowledge. You work for it. It comes from relentless effort. It can be tedious and tiring. Knowledge isn't a gift."

"I thought you said it would be exciting," says Hester.

"It's a special kind of excitement," says Howe. "It's the thrill of the hunt, the love of discovery. And it's not *just* hard work. If acquiring knowledge was only a matter of hard work, we'd already know everything. Knowledge is curiously elusive."

> To transmit values, focus on stories with meaning for the here and now.

"Why is that?" asks Sandra.

"The trouble is," says Howe, "we know more than we can tell. Much of our knowledge is invisible to us. And even worse: most of what we think we know is false and has to be unlearned. Knowledge is more fugitive than any wild animal. It has to be tracked and stalked and hunted. It requires infinite cunning and subtlety and stealth."

"I suspect you're making it more complex than it really is," says Mark.

"The world's a complex place," says Howe. "We know more than we can tell. There are many things we do to make sense of the world, and to get around in it, that we can't explain or describe."

Recognize that high-value knowledge is partly tacit.

"Are you saying," says Hester, "that we don't know what we know?"

"We may not be able to explain our knowledge," says Howe. "We're acquiring knowledge all the time in our interactions with the world. Once we master something, our minds put that knowledge aside and turn their attention elsewhere. We internalize our knowledge and the mind moves it out of sight. For a narrative to capture and transfer our knowledge to others, it has to reflect not just the knowledge we're aware of but also those practices that have become invisible to us. This is tricky."

"And strange," says Sandra.

"It gets stranger," says Howe. "A lot of what we know about any explanation is distributed across many individuals. No single individual knows it all. It lies in the community mind."

A robust knowledge-sharing story is developed with the aid of multiple perspectives.

"Next you'll be telling us to hire some experts," says Mark.

"Expertise isn't bad," says Howe, "when it's based on genuine knowledge. You shouldn't limit yourself to a single field of expertise. Genuine knowledge is multifaceted. If you get stuck with a single field of expertise, you'll never achieve more than partial understanding."[2]

"You also said that most of what we think we know is wrong," says Sandra.

"We're like the chicken who thought the farmer was feeding her out of the goodness of his heart," says Howe. "We're drowning in false knowledge. Everywhere there are pundits, gurus, and consultants, all spouting theories, all claiming to know so much, yet all delivering so little. It's opinion and spin, promise without performance, accounts without accountability."

"Why is that?" asks Mark.

"Like the chicken," says Howe, "we lack the mental toughness to confront the bad news. The chicken was happy to see her food coming reliably each day. Once she found a simple explanation, she never thought more about it. The repetition of good news dulled her senses and lulled her into complacency. Each day her meal came, she grew more confident that the farmer desired her welfare. She saw nothing to worry about, nothing to ignite new insight.

A knowledge-sharing story confronts the bad news, finding the sweet spot of learning between disaster and pure success.

"If she'd noticed that something was amiss, for instance that her fellow chickens were disappearing one by one from the coop, she might have learned something. Understanding comes from spotting a problem or an obstacle. A difficulty or concern stimulates us to solve the problem. It catalyzes understanding.

"But the chicken waited until there was total disaster, when she herself was killed and eaten. By then it was too late to learn. In a disaster the best we can do is to send in inspectors or detectives to view the remains and learn what can be inferred.

"There's a sweet spot of learning in the middle— between complete success at one end and utter disaster at the other. It's the near misses and the things that go slightly amiss—the mild problems—that's the area of high learning for all of us."

"You're saying, 'Focus on the bad news'?" asks Sandra.

"Right," says Howe.

"How depressing!" says Hester.

"On the contrary," says Howe. "If we're depressed, it's because our ignorance has rendered us helpless. Once we understand our difficulties and master them, then we can progress. Just as inertia produces despair, so understanding gives us hope. With understanding, life can begin to mend. We can emerge from our role as victims. We find a gateway to make our lives whole again."

"Surely we can also learn something from our successes," says Sandra.

"In our successes," says Howe, "we forget the elements that led to success. Once a problem is solved, we put it out of mind. When we reach our goal, all those steps along the way are forgotten. Yet *how* we solved those problems is the genuine knowledge. That's what's happened in Squirrel Inc. We've forgotten the very technology that made nut burying a success."

"That's it?" I say.

"Saving Squirrel Inc. entails gathering the narratives that embody genuine knowledge," says Howe. "These are stories with a problem, a setting, a solution, and an explanation. They are very different from folk tales or jokes. The explanations are checked and verified as being the best available. They reflect multiple perspectives and draw on serendipity. They are focused on a specific knowledge goal. They are problem oriented and are most likely to be fertile when they are located in the sweet spot between disaster and success. If we do this carefully and well, I see no problem for the future."

There is a silence of some seconds, as though the audience hardly knows what to make of Howe's presentation, delivered in his rapid-fire style.

"As usual, Howe was very impressive," says Sandra quietly. "But personally I'm confused. Just a minute ago, Mocha had me convinced that it's while we're smiling that we comprehend reality in all its flowing holistic complexity. Now Howe has me thinking exactly the opposite: finding the truth lies in painstaking attention to the details of the bad news. Which is it?"

> A knowledge-sharing story is a true story, focused on a problem and including the setting, the solution, and an explanation of the solution.

"Let's not confuse joking with knowing," says Howe. "Comic relief is fleeting because we are deceived. When we laugh, we delude ourselves that the whole world is in our hands; but when the joke's over, we discover it's slipped through our fingers. The laughter passes and we wake up, back in reality. The hard problems are still there. It's infantile to think that ridiculing our difficulties will get them fixed. Quite the opposite. By mocking our problems we defer any learning, and that makes them worse. The truth is, humor is a refuge for feeble minds. Comedy distorts, confuses, exaggerates, and in the end defrauds."

"What do you say to that, Mocha?" asks Sandra.

"You could have fooled me!" says Mocha.

"That's all?" says Sandra.

"Howe is like one of those squirrels," says Mocha, "who arrives at the birdfeeder with a great deal of noise and an immense amount of equipment—sticks, stones, the works—and after a vast amount of time and trouble and commotion, ends up unable to get access."

"You can't criticize what you don't understand," says Howe.

"What's the point?" says Mocha. "You're so caught up in tiny truths, you'll never see the trees for the leaves."

"Unfortunately," says Howe, "you'll never understand either."

"Whether either view is important," says Sandra, "depends on where you're heading."

"Why don't you tell us where we're heading?" I say, beckoning for her to take the floor.

USING STORYTELLING
TO SHARE KNOWLEDGE
Guidelines

All knowledge is ultimately based on experience, and narratives are the vehicle by which that experience is transmitted from one person to another. Easy to overlook, the knowledge-sharing story is the uncelebrated workhorse of narrative— unashamedly unentertaining but eternally useful.

Knowledge-sharing narratives have several unusual aspects. Often they lack a hero or heroine or a detectable plot. Knowledge-sharing narratives are about *problems* and how they got—or didn't get—to be resolved and why. These narratives typically contain the *context,* the *solution,* and most important, the *explanation,* which tells why the solution had the effect that it did. What was the mechanism underlying the result? Any set of observations is compatible with multiple explanations. The knowledge-sharing story provides the best explanation for the desired result.[3]

Because knowledge-sharing narratives are about problems, they typically have a *negative tone.* Knowledge-sharing stories are stories about issues and difficulties and how they were dealt with. In an organization much of the challenge in sharing knowledge lies in creating settings that enable staff to talk about what has gone wrong and how it can be fixed. In a corporate setting, stories about problems don't flow easily, not only because of the *fear of repercussions* from admitting mistakes but also because, in the flush of success, people *tend to forget* what they learned along the way. As a result the knowledge-sharing story cannot be compelled: it has to be teased out.

Methods for Teasing Out the Knowledge-Sharing Story[4]
- Confront the knower with new problems: because we only know what we know when we need to know it, a new problem can stimulate recall of what a person knows.
- Use "open space" meetings to encourage different perspectives.
- Get people to talk about the matter rather than write

about it: it's a shorter distance from the mind to the lips than from the mind to the fingers.

- Conduct a what-if discussion: "What if we'd done this?" or, "What if we hadn't done that?" Even though it's not about what actually happened, this discussion may indirectly reveal genuine knowledge.
- Awaken dormant memories through role playing.
- Enhance self-awareness by working in a cycle in which action is routinely followed by reflection.

Caveat: open access to genuine knowledge can be liberating and exhilarating as people throw off the shackles of ignorance; however, conversely, the manipulation of purported knowledge by those with ulterior motives can imprison the human spirit, condemning people to suffer the shackles of a false orthodoxy.

Chapter Nine

Sandra's Story

How to Use Storytelling to Create a Future

Cassandra had been loved by Apollo, and he gave her the gift of prophecy; but afterwards, offended with her, he rendered the gift unavailing by ordaining that her predictions should never be believed.

—THOMAS BULLFINCH

Sandra comes to the front and gives a little laugh, as if she is thinking of something delicious.

"Why are you smiling?" asks Hester.

"Everything's been so negative," says Sandra. "I'm thinking of what's to come. We've just heard that value comes from analyzing the bad news. But if we focus only on what's gone wrong, our future will also be wrong. We learn what to avoid but not where we should go. In focusing on the past we miss the possibilities.

"Always looking backward at the bad things that happened—it's pathological. If nature intended us to look backward, our eyes would be in the backs of our heads. We need stories that look forward. We need stories that make everyone say, 'Yes! I like that! Yes! That's what we need to do!'

"It's futile trying to stop bad things from happening. We solve one problem, and in the process we generate another. When we fix the things that didn't work, we find that each fix needs a new fix. So there's no end to the fixing.

"If we're going to save Squirrel Inc., we need a different way of thinking. We need to ask: How do we make things the way we want them to be? What would that be like? How can we all help create such a place?"

"Now you're talking!" says Ted, and then he turns to Diana. "Isn't that what we need for the nut-storing strategy?"

Leadership stories draw everyone into the future.

"These are stories about the future," says Sandra. "Once your stories help people picture a better state of affairs, they become willing to follow you to get there. When you have followers, you're a leader, whether you have an official position or not. I've seen top managers with no followers. I've seen individuals with no position but many followers. It's those with followers who are the real leaders."

"Yes, but how do you do it?" asks Ted. "How do you tell those kinds of stories?"

"You begin with a vision," says Sandra. "That vision is a better idea for the future. For instance, think of Diana's vision for Squirrel Inc.:

"We're going to transform Squirrel Inc. into a nut-storing organization."

"You call that a story?" says Whyse.

"It's a vision," says Sandra.

"It's not a story," says Whyse.

"Call it what you want," says Sandra. "With a vision, the question is whether it resonates. When an idea like this sidles up to us and turns disillusionment into desire, everyone's excited."

"Let's not get carried away," says Howe.

"Let's just say that it's a vision that's resonating at every level," says Sandra. "For the first time that I can remember, we have an idea in Squirrel Inc. on which the top and the bottom are both gung ho. It's simple, and it can be communicated quickly."

"I don't get it," says Whyse. "I still don't see what it means to be a nut-storing organization."

"Of course you can spell out the vision in more detail," says Sandra. "That's when it becomes a business model. That's a story that explains how Squirrel Inc. will operate if it implements the vision. The business model answers questions like: Who is the customer? And what does the customer value? How do we make money in this business? What is the underlying economic logic that shows how we can deliver value to customers at an appropriate cost?[1]

A business model is a story, set in the near future, that explains the business, who the customer is, and how the business will make money.

"Right now, squirrels are losing at least half the acorns they bury, and the percentage is steadily getting higher. What's held them back from storing more acorns has been fear of theft as well as lack of a reliable technology for a long winter. With the technology that Squirrel Inc. can offer, squirrels could store their acorns at reasonable cost, secure in the knowledge that they will get through the winter."

"Isn't this a scenario?" says Mark.

"A scenario is a story covering a longer time period," says Sandra. "A business model is a story set in the near future. In contrast, a scenario spells out the long-term implications."

"Perhaps a scenario might help me to understand it," says Whyse.

A scenario is a future story that might stretch a number of years into the future.

"The problem with a scenario," says Sandra, "is that because you craft it for a long period, it often seems unbelievable. For instance, when the nut-storing scenario was presented to Squirrel Inc. not so long ago, no one believed it. It was as if the future tripped them up. They couldn't envisage second- and third-order consequences that flowed from the idea."

"I'm sorry, my dear," says Howe, "but I can see I have to intervene. Evidently you still don't understand scenario planning. There's no need to *believe* a scenario. Scenarios are mere hypotheses. We know we can't predict the future. We use scenarios to explore a range of possibilities and prepare for whatever may happen. The credibility of any individual scenario isn't significant."

"If a scenario isn't credible," says Mark, "how can anyone select it?"[2]

"That's the problem with scenarios in general," says Sandra. "Even the team that prepares a scenario rarely believes it. Even if the scenario looks credible today, it's outdated straight away. Something happens, and everyone can see immediately that it's unbelievable. It's *science fiction*, and that isn't a compliment. That's why a future story is best when it's short and evocative. You let the listener do the work. You let the listener imagine how things will be. That's what's wonderful about Diana's vision. We can all envision different futures."

"Maybe I should set the record straight," says Howe. "I was present last year when the nut-storing scenario was rejected. The other scenarios were well fleshed out and credible. Nut storing was set aside because it was too far-fetched."

> Because future stories tend to be incredible, the future story should be short and evocative.

"The scenarios that were accepted weren't real alternatives," says Mark. "They were merely variations on the present."

"Fortunately this is ancient history," says Sandra. "As we heard at the outset, since last week, everything is different. Nut storing has become the official strategy of Squirrel Inc. The managing committee approved it. Diana here is in charge of implementing it. It's decided."

"Don't count on it," says Howe.

"What do you mean?" asks Sandra.

"I know some will be disappointed," says Howe. "I've come from a meeting with the CEO this evening. I presented the new market study that my department has just done. We interviewed fifty-six squirrels, and not one was interested in having Squirrel Inc. help him or her store acorns. Not a single one. It's an open-and-shut case. Nut storing might be fine in another time and place, but thank heaven, the CEO saw the light and put the whole thing on hold. Nut storing isn't a business for Squirrel Inc. Squirrel Inc. will go on doing the things it does best."

"The CEO bought that?" asks Diana.

"Thank heaven," says Howe. "The idea is a nonstarter. Personally I'm relieved. Squirrel Inc. was on the brink of doing something silly."

"Strange!" says Diana. "Passing strange! Only last week, the managing committee endorsed it. And just yesterday the CEO himself told me that it's his number one priority: 'the key to the future' were his very words."

"Ah, yes, the managing committee," says Howe. "That, my dear, was a fiasco. Somehow you cast a spell over otherwise sensible executives. I don't know what it was—your look, your voice, the way you held yourself, your eyes. It was a performance all right. In one golden moment, they suddenly succumbed. I've never seen anything like it. All reason evaporated. Suddenly everyone was talking about storing acorns! Extraordinary! Fortunately I could speak to the CEO more calmly this evening. I showed him the hard numbers in the market study. At last he could see that as a scenario, nut storing doesn't pass muster. As a strategy, it's a catastrophe."

"You don't think he'd speak to me," says Diana, "before reversing his decision?"

"I expect he'll explain that the game plan has changed," says Howe. "I know it's disappointing, but you'll get another position, don't worry."

"You think I want another position?" says Diana.

"Going behind her back," says Hester. "You odious rodent!"

"It wasn't just my right," says Howe. "It was my duty to tell the CEO. This isn't the time or the place to discuss Squirrel Inc.'s strategy. That's internal to Squirrel Inc. But don't be distracted by the fact that Sandra works in strategy. Squirrel Inc. isn't a nut-storing organization. I don't think it ever will be."

"You don't believe in nut storing, do you?" says Hester.

"No, I don't," says Howe.

"That's the problem with future stories," says Sandra. "They're *unbelievable*."

"Your problem, my dear, is you haven't done the numbers," says Howe. "The hard facts are there. You need to be more tough-minded. You have to grapple with the bad news."

"Could I say something?" says Diana.

"Of course," I say. "Go ahead."

"You told us earlier tonight, Howe, about the chicken who came up with the wrong explanation of why she was being fed," says Diana. "You illustrated the fallacy of induction. You told us that for every set of observations, there's always more than one possible explanation, right?"

"Correct," says Howe. "The poor chicken got it wrong."

"And now you've just interviewed fifty-six squirrels," says Diana, "and none of them can see the role of Squirrel Inc. in helping them store acorns?"

"None," says Howe.

"The explanation that you've drawn from this is that no squirrel will ever use Squirrel Inc. for storing acorns," says Diana.

"Precisely," says Howe.

"But perhaps there's another explanation," says Diana.

"I don't see it," says Howe.

"Perhaps," says Diana, "these fifty-six squirrels that you interviewed couldn't imagine what it would be like to store acorns instead of burying them. Perhaps they weren't aware of the storage technology that Squirrel Inc. could offer. Perhaps you didn't tell them what that technology was. Perhaps they couldn't see how cheap and easy it would be. Perhaps they didn't dream how this could transform their lives."

"If the market isn't there," says Howe, "no amount of dreaming will create it."

"How do we know that the market isn't there?" says Diana. "Your hard numbers are about the past. The future can't be scrutinized. It hasn't happened yet. It doesn't have any hard numbers. You've never seen a nut-storing organization. Neither have those fifty-six squirrels you interviewed. So when you ask them whether they'd be interested in such an organization or the services it could provide, naturally they say no. They can't imagine it. They can't visualize what it would be like to have an organization that could help them store their acorns safely and securely at a reasonable price. You're focused only on the world as it already exists. You're just like the chicken who committed the fallacy of induction. Your numbers are hard, but they're all about the past. Your interpretation of the future is not only soft. It's wrong!"

"If you believe that," says Howe, "you'll believe any-thing. Anyway it's late, and I'm afraid I have to be on my way."

With that, Howe rushes out of the tavern, leaving everyone stunned.

"What was all that about?" I say finally.

"It's not about nut storing," says Diana. "Howe's against *all* change. He lost out in the managing committee; now he's done an end-run."

"What does the meeting with the CEO mean?" asks Ted.

"I'll speak to him tomorrow," says Diana. "I've read Howe's market study. It's based on what squirrels currently know about burying acorns. It doesn't tell us how they'd respond if they could get genuine help with nut-storing technology."

Unlike an explanation that tries to close things down, a future story opens up possibilities.

"Imagine him dropping his bombshell," says Whyse, "and then heading off!"

"Typical muskrat tactic," says Diana.

"We're expected to accept his study," says Hester, "and go home?"

"Howe would steal flies from a blind spider," says Mocha.

"It's the technique of the pseudo-expert," says Sandra. "Howe claims to have the winning expertise. End of story. Checkmate. Game over. Back to the status quo. He's trying to bully us into silence and close things down.

"In contrast, a vision opens things up. A vision invites us to discuss. Whether a vision will crystallize depends on whether it resonates.

"Howe doesn't want resonance. He wants amplification. He wants his voice to be so loud that no one else can be heard, like a loudspeaker that we listen to not because we want to hear it but because we have no choice. Eventually it becomes noise."

"Howe is playing the knowledge game," says Hester.

"Yes," says Sandra, "but in a disreputable way. Think about his own principles! He said to look at all the possibilities and get multiple viewpoints and expect serendipity. But when it comes to actual practice, what does he do? He jumps right to the very conclusion that he's already identified."

"Scandalous," says Hester.

A successful future story fuses memory and desire.

"Happens all the time," says Mark. "That's the way the knowledge game is played. It's the gap between theory and practice."

"Howe wants to herd us into the corral of his specialist expertise," says Sandra. "We're meant to accept him as the expert. His explanation wins. Everyone else loses. It's combative and it's adversarial.

"We're meant to see Squirrel Inc. through the lens of his market study. He says it's about finding the truth, but in fact it's about getting his own way. When it comes to the crunch, the knowledge game often turns out to be about power.

"In contrast, a vision doesn't use these exclusionary moves. It doesn't claim to be true or false. It offers you a possibility. It bids you escape from the constraints of the past and enter fresh territory. It opens up a landscape of possibilities still to come.

"What Howe doesn't see, or doesn't want to see, is that the future isn't fixed and determined by the past. It's permeable, emergent, and open to the mind's causal influence. Our reality is reconstructed through new narratives. That's how the world evolves. Conscious evolution is always an option. It's the most valuable thing we do.

> Organizations are driven by stories about what the future might be.

"A future narrative acts as a magnet. It pulls the listener into the future and reverses the direction of causality."

"So what are the characteristics of a future story?" I prompt.

"It's an evocative story," says Sandra. "It's very different from knowledge sharing: it takes into account the bad news, but it's positive in orientation.

"Above all, it's a story that resonates. It's told and retold so it becomes part of the common mind. It's the unified expression of many voices playing on the same theme.

"I agree with Howe in one thing. A vision is a dream, but it's a dream with a twist: it's a dream that's shared. When we dream alone, it's just a dream. When we dream together, it's already the beginning of a new reality. When we share the same dream, we all begin to participate in it.[3]

> A future story is positive, is evocative, and resonates with listeners.

"For me, a vision is sufficient. Others may need more detail. They may need to see the 'how' of the dream. What

111

would it be like? What preparations would have to be made? How and when would they be executed? How would we overcome the problems that have undermined other companies with similar visions? Business models and scenarios can answer these questions. They put flesh on the vision. They give granularity to the plan.

"Whatever the level of detail, an effective vision results in listeners saying to themselves, 'Yes! That's what we want!' It tells us about the world as it might be in the future and helps us constitute that future."

Sandra sits down amid raucous applause.

USING STORYTELLING TO CREATE A FUTURE
Guidelines

Leadership involves taking a group of people from where they are now to where they need to be. In principle, the best way to get human beings to venture into future terrain is to make that terrain familiar and desirable by taking them there first in their imaginations through a story.[4] One would therefore expect successful leaders to create and use future stories to help people break away from the familiar present and venture boldly ahead to create a different and better future.

There is however a difficulty: how does one craft a credible narrative about the future when the future is unknowable?[5] Future narratives thus tend to be inherently unbelievable. Even if a future narrative is plausible when created, some unexpected event typically occurs to make it obvious that the future will not unfold as envisaged. So, although future narratives are potentially very valuable, it is hard to capitalize on their value.

Successful future narratives thus tend to be *brief* and *evocative:*

Winston Churchill: "We shall fight on the beaches . . ."
Martin Luther King Jr.: "I have a dream . . ."
John Fitzgerald Kennedy: "This nation should commit itself to achieving the goal, before this decade is out, of landing a man on the moon . . ."

Future narratives sketch a vision that points in a general direction but little else. If these narratives are effective, it is because the listeners themselves put flesh on the skeleton: the listeners contribute the narrative detail, prompted by the evocative narrative of the leader. This form of narrative has the advantage that as the future actually unfolds, with all its unexpected twists and turns, people can remold the narrative in their imaginations on the fly. An evocative narrative is thus continuously updated in the context as it evolves.

Caveat: the telling of an evocative future narrative requires a high degree of linguistic skill that not every leader possesses. A less exacting challenge is for leaders to use a *springboard story,* which is a story about the past—something that has actually happened—that creates a narrative about the future in the mind of the listener. Because it's very easy to tell a story about the past, a springboard story will be a more practical option for many leaders.[6]

HOWE UPSETS THE ACORNS

How Individuals and Organizations React to Change

The art of the possible is a perilous art.
It must take heed of life as we know it,
yet alienate us from it sufficiently to tempt us
into thinking of alternatives beyond it.
—JEROME BRUNER

"Now what?" says Ted. "This puts us in a difficult situation."

"Howe has upset the acorns," says Mark.

"And I had the press releases ready," says Ted wistfully.

"What will happen now?" asks Hester.

Just then Mocha gets to his feet and declares: "Distinguished friends and colleagues! It's obvious what's going to happen. Don't you see? It's as depressing as it is predictable. Just look at our history: Squirrel Inc. will continue as is."

"How can it?" asks Sandra. "We know that will be a disaster."

"Like the other corporations that went before it," says Mocha, "Squirrel Inc. sees the looming catastrophe. But like the sorcerer's apprentice, it persists, with ever-increasing energy, in what worked for it in the past. It works hard rather than smart.

"I doubt whether we'll ever totally reject the nut-storing strategy. It's one of the things we'll go on considering but without ever coming to a clear-cut decision. We'll muddle along, neither wholeheartedly accepting the idea nor entirely rejecting it. The firm may never totally collapse, but it will never do really well, all the time grinding itself deeper into the rut in which it is stuck.

"The thing is this. It's difficult for a firm like Squirrel Inc. to make a basic change in its core business strategy, particularly since it's been pursuing that strategy for decades. Standard ways of doing things have become embedded in the minds and hearts of everyone who works here. Even if a better idea comes along, it's crushed by the system."

"This is simply Howe up to his old tricks," says Sandra. "This can be fixed."

"Maybe you can fix Howe," says Mocha, "but then something else will happen. If it isn't Howe doing an end-run to the CEO, it'll be someone else who has the old way of doing things engrained in his soul and knows in his heart that deviating from the past is somehow wrong, almost immoral. He'll find a way to subvert the change and keep Squirrel Inc. safely and surely on its original course."

Then Diana breaks in: "I'm sorry, Mocha, but that is too cynical. Think about what we've listened to tonight. Not only do we have a genuinely better idea for the future of Squirrel Inc., we have the tools to communicate it and the know-how to use them."

"How would that happen?" asks Mocha, reaching once more for his woodcup.

"Let's think," says Diana. "Let's work backward. Let's imagine that it's six months down the pike. Let's imagine that Squirrel Inc. has indeed succeeded. Let's imagine that we have made the transition from a nut-burying to a nut-storing organization. What will have happened to enable this transformation to take place?[1]

"Thanks to our bartender, we already know how a story can be used to spark change. I'll speak to the CEO tomorrow. Since we have a good idea and the tool to communicate it, I have no doubt in my ability to instill in him the vision for the new Squirrel Inc. and his role in it."

> A leader uses storytelling to communicate a bold new idea.

"That's just the beginning of the difficulty," says Mocha. "A CEO is always ready to talk about change. It's the hard-core resistance below him that's the problem."

"I agree, it's a beginning," says Diana. "But it's a good place to start. So we begin by undoing the mischief that Howe has instigated. The CEO knows that continuing as we are isn't an option. Nut burying worked for us in the past, but it isn't a solution for the future.

"Clearly he's got to learn what I've learnt—how to communicate the change idea through a story. Maybe he'll ask me to teach him. Maybe he'll figure it out for himself simply by listening to me. Either way, if Squirrel Inc.

is going to make the transition, the CEO himself needs to become a persuasive advocate of change.

"Second, the CEO needs to get everyone working together. Clearly Howe isn't the only one who feels run over. Objectively we all have an interest in making nut storing work. But Howe and the others have to see that for themselves. If they sit in their corners nursing their wounds, the wounds will fester and eventually break out into the open again, perhaps when we least need it. So just as Hester recommends, the CEO needs to get the teams together and have the members share their stories, so they start to see who they are as individuals and understand each other's perspectives. Then these groups will have a shared interest in seeing the idea succeed. We'll use storytelling to get everyone working together.

A leader uses storytelling to get people working together.

"I can't see Howe," says Mocha, "falling for rah-rah camaraderie."

"Storytelling doesn't work on everyone," says Diana. "Not someone stuck in the current story. Maybe Howe has to be let go if he can't manage the shift. You can't have one staff member jeopardizing the whole firm."

A leader can use satire to ridicule the opposition into oblivion.

"Keep in mind, Howe is not alone," says Mocha. "Other diehards will be undermining the change at every turn."

"Right," says Diana. "There's a hard core of resistance, and the CEO needs to deal with it. But there are things he can do."

"Like what?" asks Mocha.

"For one thing," says Diana. "The CEO can take a page out of your book, Mocha, and use satire. He can satirize the resisters as doddering old fogies. He can mock them into adopting the change idea. He can shame them into changing.

A leader uses future stories to lead people into the future.

"And Sandra can teach him how to tell future stories. To inspire a new vision maybe we can come up with something that is evocative enough so that it sings to the spirit.

"Even Howe himself has a lot to offer. For instance, knowledge-sharing stories can help disseminate the technology we'll need for nut storing. This is a new field for Squirrel Inc., and we'll have to innovate quickly. Knowledge-sharing stories will be crucial in capturing and transferring new knowledge as it's created.

"The CEO also needs to learn how to project himself as a leader by telling stories that communicate who he is. Just as Whyse suggested, he'll have to tell his personal story so that we all understand his character. Then he'll be a distinct individual, not just a cog filling a slot.

A leader uses storytelling to transmit knowledge.

"And Ted can use stories about Squirrel Inc. to enhance our brand. We're not just a nut-burying company.

We're a company that ensures that squirrels always have food. The brand is aimed at those outside the firm, but it will also help those inside to focus.

A leader uses storytelling to communicate his or her personal identity.

"So, if Squirrel Inc. is going to survive, as I think it will, it will do so with the tools that we've talked about here tonight. We have the individuals on hand who understand the magic of narrative. So if we use this understanding, we've got what we need to prevail."

"It's one hell of an agenda," says Mocha.

"That's what it'll take to save this great old corporation," says Diana.

"You're saying that the CEO magically acquires these new skills?" says Whyse.

"Actually they're not new skills," says Diana. "The CEO already has them. Storytelling is innate in us all. What we'll be doing is reminding him of what he has always known but somehow forgotten."

A leader uses storytelling to communicate the firm's identity.

"You're expecting a lot from a CEO who's never shown any inclination to learn," says Whyse.

"It's what he'll have to do to lead," says Diana. "If he doesn't, he's history."

"Well, let's accept for a second that Squirrel Inc. implements the change," says Whyse. "My worry is a different one. My concern is whether the change is safe. Just think about it. Squirrels perform a key environmental function by burying nuts and then losing them. That's how forests regenerate themselves. If the squirrels stop doing that, the impact from implementing the new strategy could be massive. If Squirrel Inc. interferes with the environmental cycle, then Squirrel Inc. might be on a disaster path that is even worse than its current one."

"You see, my fellow squirrels," says Mocha. "Skeptics, in our very midst!"

"What about forests where there are no squirrels?" says Diana. "Have you ever thought how those forests regenerate themselves?"

"I'm worried about this particular ecosystem," says Whyse. "That's all."

Then Sandra speaks up. "This discussion is both too optimistic and too pessimistic. On the one hand I agree with Mocha that Diana has a problem. She's bright. She's sharp. She's better than the CEO. In other words she's a threat to him, and he will treat her like one. In a real organizational transformation, not a mere change in leadership, the best individuals, unfortunately, don't typically end up on top. It would be nice if they did. But they don't. It's often hypocrites like Howe who grab the levers of power. The courageous and noble may begin the movement, but they soon become its victims. That's the nature of transformation.

"On the other hand I don't agree with my good friend, Whyse the worrywart, that nut storing isn't a good idea. I think it's an excellent idea. Squirrel Inc. can generate resources by helping squirrels store nuts, through the sale of good tools and the provision of services. The environment will survive.

"No, my concern lies elsewhere. Just look at Squirrel Inc. What kind of company is it? It's traditional. It's slow. It's boring. Do we have to take this? Do we have to stick around and kowtow to the resisters and put up with the naysayers while Squirrel Inc. goes down the tubes?

"Initially it may break our hearts that the nut-storing vision doesn't get accepted at Squirrel Inc., but do we have to endure this and die from broken hearts? No! If Squirrel Inc. won't embrace nut storing, then forget Squirrel Inc.! Let's form our own company so we can do the right thing from the get-go."

At this point things become unruly as the discussion breaks up into private conversations. Amidst the hubble-bubble over Howe's intervention, suddenly a new band of squirrels comes in and adds to the ruckus. In the confusion that ensues, Diana slips away, as it's obvious that there'll be no more substantive discussion tonight. Everyone who stays ends up drinking large quantities of extra-ferments.

REACTING TO CHANGE
Guidelines

When an organization in decline is faced with a bold and disruptive change proposal that could transform its future, several outcomes are possible.

Four Typical Scenarios
Scenario 1. The organization never formally rejects the change proposal. It is unable to make a clear-cut decision to accept it or reject it. It muddles along in a cycle of decline, neither wholeheartedly embracing the new idea

nor entirely rejecting it, all the time grinding itself deeper into the rut in which it is stuck.[2]

Scenario 2. The organization implements the change idea, but it turns out that the idea doesn't work. The organization then finds itself on a disaster path that is even worse than the track it was on before.[3]

Scenario 3. The organization gradually shifts to the new strategy—not decisively but in a slow, agonizing process. Key employees become impatient with the glacial pace of change and quit the firm to set up their own organization, which becomes a direct competitive threat to the parent company.[4]

Scenario 4. The leadership successfully engineers a turnaround, using means that include communicating the new strategy and sparking action toward implementation, getting individuals to work together, neutralizing the grapevine, sharing knowledge about new technology for implementing the change, communicating who the organization's leaders really are, and publicizing the firm's brand. In all these areas storytelling can play a role, because a psychological turnaround must precede the actual change.[5]

PART THREE

I can only answer the question
"What am I to do?"
if I can answer the prior question
"Of what story do I find myself a part?"
—ALASDAIR MACINTYRE

Chapter Eleven

THE JOURNEY
OF A LEADER

Staying Alive Through
the Dangers of Leadership

The deeper the change and the greater the
amount of new learning required,
the more resistance there will be and, thus,
the greater the danger to those who lead.
—RONALD HEIFETZ AND MARTY LINSKY

E very part of the day has its merits, but I prefer the time
around five o'clock in the afternoon when I'm putting
the final touches on the bar for the evening rush, which
tonight as it happens is strangely late in coming. The discussion of a couple of nights ago is still ringing in my ears. As I
think back on it, it was as if—at least for one evening—we had
glimpsed possibilities with no limit: it was exhilarating to
think of the future Squirrel Inc. could have if those insights
were implemented. And yet how impotent these insights were
and what little chance there was of realizing the possibilities
in the face of the inevitable bad faith!

Everything that's happened since fits that familiar pattern. When Diana got to see the CEO the next day, he did no more than listen politely. Although she was upbeat about the meeting and said things would be sorted out, she hasn't heard anything since, and the atmosphere has become anxious. I'm an outsider and I've observed so many corporate crises in my time that I won't be too grieved if the grim predictions materialize: Squirrel Inc.'s future isn't my business. It's a game I've chosen not to play. I have my tavern high up in a green and leafy oak tree on 44th Street. What more do I need in life? And besides, the bigger the crisis, the higher the demand for extra-ferments.

My ruminations are interrupted when six large and intimidating squirrels fill the doorway of my tavern. From their looks I know they're not here to sip my celebrated rose nectar. As they make their way into the bar, one of them proceeds to drag his freshly sharpened claws over my newly polished tables. As I move to confront him, an empty woodcup flies within inches of my ears and smashes the mirror behind me. All hell breaks loose, and I retreat behind the bar. Why is this happening? My newly purchased woodcups are hurled across the room, fresh jars of nectar are smashed, and precious extra-ferment is poured all over the floor.

My fear and confusion soon turns to fury as my instincts kick in and I remember what it means to be a squirrel. As I emerge from behind the bar, I have the strength of several and focus my energy on the leader, who is also the smallest of the bunch. I'm about to do something terrible to him when a pair of large guards intervene. They overpower me and pin me down. The chief stands over me. He tells me that my bar is a haven for subversives.

I ask whether that's any reason to tear the place apart.
He has the guards throw me out.

"This can't be happening," I think as I pick myself
up. The pain in my hip convinces me it is.

Who are they? Where are they from? It doesn't take
me more than an instant to figure it out: Squirrel Inc.! Somehow I've now become part of the drama. In a panic I run this
way and that, desperate to find someone who can fill me in,
tell me what's going on.

Finally, I stumble on Mocha. He's asleep, and looks
very disheveled. He wouldn't be my first choice as a witness,
but what option do I have? I shake him till he is awake and
tell him what's been done to my bar.

He stares at me for a while. Then he says: "So the
lizards in Squirrel Inc. finally got to you too?"

When I press him to tell me what happened earlier
in the day, he says it went like this. That afternoon, the CEO
had suddenly called a meeting of senior staff, all hands on
deck. All the grand maharajas of management were there.
Not just the new CEO but the old CEO as well. Howe was
sitting up front with them. Not a good sign. He was trying to
suppress a wide smile. More bad news. No sign of Diana.
Definitely trouble. Ted was fluttering about like a troubled
butterfly.

The CEO began by saying that there had been a lot
of misguided talk about a shift in Squirrel Inc.'s strategy.
Irresponsible talk about becoming a nut-storing company.
In the future, he said, all this talk had got to stop. Nut storing wasn't going to happen. That was final. Squirrel Inc. had
always been a nut-burying company. That was its focus. That
was its goal. The little diversion into nut storing was over.

Management had considered it. It wasn't going to work. It was time to move on.

Then he announced that Diana was quitting the firm to pursue other career opportunities. Who was he trying to fool? For heaven's sake, why couldn't he tell it like it is for once? She was canned! He also lowered the boom on Sandra's strategy department. It was being folded into the budgeting group. Howe was the new vice president. The CEO also announced that the nectar bar was off limits. Then, being an open, participative manager, he asked whether there were any questions.

After all that had been said in the bar that night about supporting Diana, did anyone stand up and utter even a squeak on her behalf? No, nothing. Remember how many Squirrel Inc. staffers had said they were on her side? Mark. Hester. Sandra. A bunch of them. Now all they could manage was sullen compliance with the management diktat.

I ask Mocha whether he had said anything. He says he was grabbing forty winks by that time.

I thank him and wander onward, struggling to make sense of it. One thing is sure: if my nectar bar is off limits to Squirrel Inc. employees, business will be difficult even if I can put it together again. Who will I have as clients? I've never done Squirrel Inc. any harm. Now that it's on the skids, it's blasting at irrelevant targets. Diana. Sandra. And more to the point, me. Instead of focusing on the real problem—the failing business model—it's taking aim at scapegoats.

Next I run into Ted and ask him what went wrong. He says the signals have shifted; it's a done deal. Why try fighting? We've got to move on.

I move on to see if I can find Diana. I wander all over because I'd never bothered to ask her where she lives. But finally I find her, residing in a neat little setup not far from my bar.

I should have guessed. Despite everything, she's in excellent spirits. She has a plan to fight back. She's going to talk to the board members, one by one. She'll find the employees who are on her side. She's got a business model and budget ready to go. She's pumped up and full of energy. Her eyes are shining. There's a lilt in her voice. She isn't fazed by the apparent setbacks. In fact when she talks of these matters her intensity is evangelical.

But over the next few days all she encounters are roadblocks and blind alleys. The CEO, with Howe's help, has turned her into a persona non grata. Most board members won't talk to her, and those that do are not forthcoming. Even her old colleagues are reluctant to be seen with her. In effect the doors of Squirrel Inc. have clanged shut in her face.

Yet she doesn't lose her enthusiasm. She's down, but by God, she's not out. Her career in Squirrel Inc. may be over. But not her future in nut storing. Getting fired is a blessing in disguise. Now that she's resolved the financial and technical issues of nut storing, she'll start her own firm. She'll take the best and the brightest with her. She'll do what Squirrel Inc. lacks the sense to do.

Good thinking—until she tries to implement it. When she invites her colleagues to join her, she finds they're unwilling to take the risk. They're frightened for their livelihood. Earlier, when she was promoting the nut-storing strategy and she looked like a winner, she had enormous support.

131

Nothing was too much trouble. Now that she's on the outside it's a whole different story.

You might have thought that Mark and Hester would be willing. Hadn't they talked about values? The importance of working together? Remember that? Well, they also politely decline, pointing to the lack of market.

"Of course there's no market," says Diana. "There's never a market when you're starting. We're going to create the market. It's already happened in the Windy City."

But it's no use. Mark and Hester have families, and they're not willing to run the risk. Sandra might have considered leaving since she's already been set aside. But suddenly Squirrel Inc. gives her a formal reprimand for discussing company strategy in public and says that if she quits now her severance pay will be annulled. And so even she says that she won't be able to join Diana at this time.

Some help comes from a source you'd never suspect: Mocha. Despite his bluster he's the one with the guts to do something. But Diana will need more than Mocha to launch her firm. The difficulties of assembling talent cause her financing plan to unravel, and her start-up looks like an uphill climb. Then her home is burglarized.

On my side, I quietly explore the idea of reopening my bar farther away from Squirrel Inc., but my news is just as discouraging. Even if my place is located farther away, I still don't think my old clients will come.

Just when I think things couldn't be worse, I suffer a hammer blow: Dio has been killed. It is something more, and something less, than an accident. I'm afraid she'd lost her way and spent her time meditating on the meaning of existence. She would stop dead in her tracks when some new insight struck her, as she plumbed its unexpected meanings. One morning she was making her way along a fence when a puzzling problem suddenly occurred to her, and she stopped there, fixated, thinking about it. She was still in this position, meditating, when she was sprung upon by a large cat and torn to pieces, limb from limb.

This new calamity sends me into a deep depression for more than a week. Although I hadn't seen Dio for months, she'd never been far from my thoughts. Her quick wit and her storytelling performances were an inspiration. Now that she's gone, I do nothing but think about the contribution she could have made if she'd not gone on the road.

• • •

It's at this moment Diana asks me to come with her to the Windy City. The suggestion is so unexpected and her tone so sternly purposeful that initially I miss the compassion that lies behind her request. Her intentions are hidden inside the seeming strength of all that up-front explicitness about the length of the journey, the effort involved, the places we would stay, the sights to see, and the measures needed to protect ourselves. I realize that I still don't know much about this svelte ex-exec.

I look her in the eye. It's a long journey for a female. Even though she's small and delicately put together, she looks durable. I'm generally considered a tough old buzzard, and I can see why she thinks I might be helpful on such an expedition. Apparently Sandra had planned to go with her, but now she can't make the trip. Would I be willing to come?

I can think of a million reasons not to. For one thing the trip is long and risky. Diana says exciting things are happening in the Windy City that she needs to see for herself. It's the next step in some labyrinth she's navigating. I really don't get it. If only she could unbend a little! If she wants to hook up with Skip again, that is none of my business.

But then again, I'm also thinking there's no particular reason to stay where I am. My bar is closed and I can't see how to reopen it. With Dio gone I don't have the energy even to think about it. This will be a perilous journey, but anyway it's getting to be unsafe staying here. I think to myself, "The ordinary air is good by nature, but when so much is going wrong, it's not a bad idea to vary it." So against my better judgment, I tell her I'll come.

● ● ●

It's about five o'clock in the afternoon, early autumn, with the sun not shining and a look of hard, wet rain in a pewter sky when we leave. Diana has told all her friends that she is leaving, but there is no one to see us off. We slip away as dusk settles on the forest. For such hazardous traveling, it's safer to go by night. I can't help thinking I'm on a fool's errand.

The immense journey has to be accomplished on the strength of our legs. As expected, Diana has everything planned down to the last detail, which I'm pleased to see she doesn't bother me with. This is a fine time of year to be on the move. Not too hot and not too cold, the air is brisk and stimulating. There are plentiful berries to be scavenged along the way, in addition to the birdfeeders.

At first we make our way through suburban back-yards. Vast tracts of development houses that look as though nobody lives in them. Urban traffic to be negotiated. Turnpikes to be crossed. Malls to be circumvented. Dogs to be run from. Raccoons to be placated. Cats to be anticipated. Hawks and owls to be avoided. There are perils everywhere. I smell the odd fox.

As we move through the countryside, suburban back-yards gradually turn into fields of corn and vegetables. We move through clumps of broom and bramble and the occasional wild thistle. We crawl past dry stone walls, wary of rats as big as weasels leaping out of trashcans. Occasionally some friendly squirrels share with us a place to stay.

After a long night of steady travel up a steep incline, it is good to look out over a fresh landscape at daybreak. After a cold fall night, the warm sun rises over the dawn mist curled like a bridal veil over the valley below. I stop to watch the sunrise, but Diana, as always obsessed with her schedule, wants to move on.

We pass through a marshland that is a paradise for blackbirds, woodpeckers, and field sparrows. It's good to be away from the city and inhaling the pungent smell of decaying vegetation, of ooze, of wilderness.

The second week is one of freezing weather followed by occasional rains and steaming mists and then gorgeous sunshine.

It is on this part of the journey, as we are making our way through the yard behind a large house, that I glimpse some of Diana's hidden abilities. We are figuring out how to break into the birdfeeder hanging from a clothesline, when we see a huge Doberman flying toward us, barking and snarling. I've never liked Dobermans, with their short shiny coats, clipped ears, and iron musculature; they combine the fire and lightning reactions of the terrier with the cunning of the guard breeds. I accept that dogs love to chase squirrels, but Dobermans have an intensity that is demented.

This crazed animal is racing toward us at a terrifying pace. Diana leaps to safety up a convenient ash tree, but in the panic of the moment I stumble and lose my footing. Before I can right myself, the Doberman is on me and its jaws are around my leg. Just as the monster is about to clamp down and snap off my limb, I realize that I am about to die. But Diana sees what is happening and leaps onto the Doberman's back. She bites his ear with such force that he yelps in pain and lets go of my leg, losing all interest in either of us. Diana leaps off his back, and we both scramble to safety up the handy ash tree.

"That was fun, wasn't it?" she says, as we sit on a branch, recovering our breath.

I don't reply, as I'm beginning to see a different individual from the young executive who waltzed into my bar some months ago. The quickness of mind to see what is happening. The nimbleness to act. The toughness to carry through her plan. It's hard even for a barman to be indifferent to someone who has just saved his life.

On the third week the journey becomes so cold and difficult that even Diana's spirits begin to wilt. Winter is coming on and intermittent patches of snow become a regular crust of ice in places. But then suddenly the air turns balmy. The wind comes from the south in sudden puffs. It is hard to think that as recently as yesterday, we considered ourselves in the grip of winter.

A few days later we enter the final stretch of the journey, through fields so vast it is difficult to determine which direction we are going. As we proceed Diana is more and more confident that we'll arrive. I have no basis for disagreeing. The strange thing is that the farther away that we are from Squirrel Inc., the better known she is and the more warmly we are greeted in the areas through which we pass.

I had thought that the real reason for the trip was that we were going to visit Skip. That is indeed still part of the story. But as the journey has progressed, I sense that if seeing Skip is part of the picture, it is not the largest part. There is a vision driving Diana onward.

When we arrive in the Windy City, I learn that her reputation has traveled before her, and the reception she gets is amazing. She has been invited—through Skip, her intermediary—to make a presentation.

After the hardships of the journey, what a contrast! Everyone seems to know who she is and what she has done. There is someone to greet her and show us where we are going to stay. The director of the event where she is to speak is genuinely pleased to see her. He offers us a drink. He inquires whether we would like anything to eat. With this kind of reception, I begin to feel the only sad thing is that we will ever have to go home.

The next day, Diana gives her speech; it centers on leadership. She gives a personal account of what she has been through and suggests that anyone with sufficient will to flourish can do so. She acknowledges the obstacles: we are victims of our ambitions; self-interest leads to self-deception; we are inconsistent, unreliable, a morass of unsatisfied appetites. But she is never despairing: we are not impotent, merely weak. We can grow stronger. We can not only aspire to what is true and worthwhile; we can even succeed in these dreams.[1]

She does not argue a case. She merely enables the listeners to relive the journey that she herself has undertaken. She speaks simply, without blame or praise, talking directly from the heart. I can see the impact when she tells her story. When they listen to her, and it doesn't matter who she's talking to, everyone is spellbound. It's not too much to say that she is the hit of the Windy City. She is besieged with offers to present elsewhere.

How different Diana is from the first time I met her! This night she has arrived. She is not only telling her story; now she is also living it.

In the days that follow she spends her time at receptions and meetings, inspecting developments in nut storing in the Windy City. Skip hangs around in the background, waiting for attention that never comes. He is also taken aback at the different individual she has become.

Eventually we have to make our way home. If we don't leave now, the bitterness of full winter will be upon us and then we won't get back before spring. When Skip says good-bye, Diana is simply polite.

● ● ●

The long journey feels shorter going back than it did in coming.

I suppose one reason is that now we know the way. Another is that we have figured out how to handle the hazards that afflict traveling squirrels.

Then something unexpected occurs when we are almost within sight of our destination. We have been warned about the risk of a flash flood, but we've seen nothing. It's almost dusk and we are moving along a dry creekbed. The dirt banks on either side are smooth and steep and overhung with protective branches. We had observed thunderstorms earlier in the afternoon, but it doesn't occur to us that they represent any threat.

Suddenly, we see a wall of water coming at us with the speed and dimensions of a freight train. Our first thought is to clamber to safety, but at this point the banks of the creek are so steep and sandy that we cannot climb high enough in time, and both of us are swept along in the onrush of the flood.

I am underwater with not the slightest idea of how to swim, but by some miracle I manage to grab a branch of a log floating by and then to haul myself on top of the log. I look around for Diana in the fading light and see that she is also hanging onto the branch for dear life. I reach out and pull her to the relative safety of the top of the log, and we clutch it desperately as it lurches and twists and turns in the onrushing flood.

We're smashing into trees, rocks, and riverbanks, and each time we take a massive jolt that almost shakes us off the log, but somehow we manage to cling on. We continue on this wild ride for I don't know how long, with our fragile lives at the mercy of the torrent.

Finally our log hits a still-rooted pine tree growing in the creekbed and then twists around and wedges itself between the tree trunk and the bank. At once we climb up and take refuge in the tree. Soaked and frightened to death we sit there, amazed at our escape.

We are silent for a time, gazing at the foaming watercourse in front of us, as we think of our strange deliverance.

I can't claim that I'm entirely responsible for saving Diana's life, but I think I did contribute.

By this time our home is no more than a night's journey away. We can even see the city's lights ahead of us. Our plan had been to push forward to our destination. But our near-drowning has been so harrowing that we decide to sleep where we are for the night instead of striking out for home.

As we are falling asleep, Diana tells me drowsily that I make a plaintive companion.

I ask her what that might mean.

She says: "I don't understand the sad tone you impose on yourself. I for one am an optimist, even if I don't have much to be optimistic about right now."

It's the first time in all these weeks that she's hinted at the difficulties awaiting her on her return. I feel a sense of protectiveness toward her, and I intuit that she is not disinterested, but it isn't anything physical.

"One day," she says, "you're going to tell me your whole god-awful history."

One day. But not today.

• • •

When we arrive in the city, she thanks me for joining her on the trip. I frankly don't know what to say. We each go our separate ways. She says she has things to attend to. God knows what.

I check in on Mocha and find him in a depressed condition. He says that things are getting steadily worse at Squirrel Inc. Its commercial returns continue their steep decline. The word is that the company will fold before the end of the year.

Mocha himself is also in bad shape. I suspect he has a great deal of talent, even if his current vocation is presenting himself as ruined.

I'm feeling done in by the journey and need time to recover. I visit my old bar, which is now boarded up. It's nostalgic to be there, remembering the good old days and looking ahead to a hideous winter.

LEADERSHIP AND RESILIENCE
Guidelines

Why do some individuals do well in life despite disappointments and misfortunes, whereas others are crushed by similar events? What makes them resilient? This critical characteristic concerns not merely getting over a single hurdle but maintaining an ongoing outlook that enables the individual to get over a succession of obstacles. Resilient individuals deal with difficult issues proactively, reframing the past and viewing the future from the point of view of its possibilities, taking the time for self-reflection, and maintaining a network of supportive relationships.[2]

No one welcomes adversity, and yet it is through adversity that we learn. It is through dealing with setbacks and obstacles that we discover ourselves—our strengths as well as our blemishes. When we know what we consist of and what we want to make of what we have, then we know who we are and we can communicate that to others.

There is something about the forge of experience that not only marks us but also affords reassurance to those we seek to lead. Why? It is through experience that we acquire balance and judgment. Experience can help us to be bold without being rash. It can assist us to recognize people's feelings without becoming soft. It may facilitate our seeing hierarchical power as a last resort rather than for routine use. It can also enable us to see mistakes and setbacks in perspective. A leader is not ashamed to admit these errors and difficulties; the only shame is not taking practical measures to remedy them. The leader is someone who has seen the meaning of what is sweet in life and what is terrible and who then goes undeterred to meet what is to come.[3]

Chapter Twelve

THE RETURN TO SQUIRREL INC.

Living the Story as Well as Telling It

Through narrative, we construct, reconstruct,
in some ways reinvent yesterday and tomorrow.
Memory and imagination fuse in the process.

—JEROME BRUNER

It is several weeks after my return from the Windy City when I hear something queer: Diana has returned to work for Squirrel Inc.

When I'm first told the news, I'm dubious. "How could she? Why would she? After all they've done to her? And Squirrel Inc.? It's on the skids! I don't get it."

"No, you don't get it," says Mocha. "She's the CEO."

"No kidding!"

"The place was in turmoil the last two weeks," says Mocha. "After another awful quarter everyone turned on the CEO and he was forced out. The board members couldn't agree on who would succeed him. Probably each of them wanted the job. Diana was the only candidate who'd both been in management and had a reputation outside Squirrel Inc. So they settled on her as the common denominator."

"Nevertheless she made it," I say.

"Yes, but the cup is poisoned," says Mocha. "The price of becoming CEO is that she's had to agree to keep the existing management team. Now she's a mouse in a snake pit. The whole thing is a setup."

That's what Mocha thinks, but I'm not so sure. It's easy to underestimate Diana. Spending time with her on our trip has given me a better sense of her character.

One evening she stops in to see me on her way home, and she asks me to reopen my bar. She says that Squirrel Inc. will reimburse me for the damage that was done when it was closed down.

I ask her whether she's bearing up. She tells me Howe is of course a problem, but he has new responsibilities. "I give him what he wants, and he gives me what he can," she says and laughs.

I'd always thought of Howe as incorrigible, but she finds ways to draw the best out of almost everyone. She's let a few individuals go, but there's something about her that makes everyone want to contribute.

"I'm counting on your help," she says.

"I don't know what I can do for you," I reply.

"You've already done a lot," she replies. "Before I met you I had success, yes. Things worked but they weren't wonderful. I functioned in a fashion. But nothing flowed. Nothing soared. I had imagined that leadership had to do with the fabrication of products, with results; that it was a drag race with winners and losers. I've come to see that those are just by-products. You can only be a leader if others believe in you. They only believe in you if you believe your own story. If the story doesn't rise up from the deepest recesses of your being, it risks being superficial and unfulfilled."

Clearly Diana has evolved. She talks of herself with an objectivity that is uncommon. There's a quiet confidence about her that I like. She stirs something inside me. It's more than friendship, but I wouldn't know what to call it. It's a pity she's so work addicted as she has a real talent for relationships. When she listens to you, she makes you feel that she is right there with you, her eyes softer and warmer than I could describe.

● ● ●

Several hectic months go by. My bar reopens, and you could almost say things are back to normal. Then Diana holds a reception and for the first time in my life, I do something I once swore I would never do: I step inside Squirrel Inc.

It's a lavish affair. Nectar. Berries. Acorns galore. All the top brass of the company on hand. Ted is presiding with a satisfied gleam of a smile.

All the regulars from my bar are there too: Mark and Hester and Whyse and Sandra.

"Poor Diana!" says Mocha, standing where the drinks are being served. "It's never going to work! Just look at her with them all. It's like driving a swarm of bees through a snowstorm without a switch."

"See, there's Howe, wending his way through the crowd!" says Hester. "Why did he survive?"

I try to avoid him but he makes a point of coming and talking to me. He is genial, relaxed, happy to concede that he may have acted badly, as he turns to sample some berries from a passing tray. He says hello to another guest, then swivels back to me to ask what else I could expect. "An end-run is the most normal thing in the world," he says, crunching on walnuts.

He acknowledges he is thought of as intellectual and cold. "The truth is I am neither."

I can't get near Diana, who is surrounded by well-wishers and pitiful strivers. But after a while she makes a speech. She talks articulately, subtly, with originality and vigor. She tells the story of our journey to the Windy City, including our encounters with the Doberman and the flash flood. She continues:

> "Why am I telling you all this? What have these stories got to do with Squirrel Inc.? In one sense, nothing. But in another, they reveal what sort of perseverance will be needed to get Squirrel Inc. through its difficulties."

Everyone listens, transfixed. In the few months that I've known her, Diana has acquired a kind of eloquence that makes one's blood stand still.

She says:

> "In all organizations there are those whose goal is merely that of control. For them the important thing is maintaining order and making reality fit the vision of yesterday. My goal here is to instigate new possibilities.
>
> "My objective is to fight for the best ideas, not to win you over to any particular side. I'm not bringing a specific nonnegotiable objective for you. Rather I want us to create our future together.

*"We're living on a threshold. It's the most exciting
and frightening place to be. Even though the old order is
dying, it still beckons us with the same melodious voice,
the harmonies we know so well.*

*"And yet a strange new order is also being born.
Its melodies are less well known and sometimes puzzling.
It's risky and unpredictable. But there's a shared understanding of what we need to do. With your help, the future
is ours."*

● ● ●

As far as the numbers go, Squirrel Inc. is still a company in
decline, but a psychological turnaround has already taken
place. There is a feeling here now that wasn't here before.
Not just on the surface of things but all through the organization.

The signs are everywhere. Morale is up. The finger
pointing has stopped. The staff believe in the future. With Diana
at the helm, almost everyone now thinks the transformation can
actually happen, and that is more than half the battle.

She still has a massive challenge. The firm has to
keep moving forward. Her game plan must succeed. Financial returns have to be generated. She has to coax the stock
price back up. The new story of Squirrel Inc. has to come
true, not just as a story but in reality. It's too early to say how
it will all turn out. Only one thing is certain: there will be
more surprises along the way.

My nectar bar is thriving again. In fact it's now a regular meeting place for Squirrel Inc. I'm holding workshops
there on an almost daily basis. It's as though my bar has been

brought within the firm. As someone from outside, I had always regarded the staff in a detached fashion, quietly smiling at the web of personal relationships and concerns in which they are all locked. Now I'm also being drawn into these orbits.

It's hard to think of myself as working for Squirrel Inc., but in practice that's what's happened. The environment is disquieting. Something has been awakened in me, but for the moment I can't put it in words. My old self-sufficient life no longer responds to my deepest needs. Somewhere inside me a tide seems to have turned. Diana's the only individual who's ever made me feel this way.

So that's where we are. We're still in midstream; life goes on. Some problems are resolved. New possibilities are unfolding. Once I would have found it difficult to admit that the future would bring anything significantly different. Now I'm not so sure. Maybe it isn't only the bright yellow crocuses of spring that make me think we're on the brink of a new beginning.

STORYTELLING
AND LEADERSHIP
Guidelines

At the heart of most books on leadership is a technological way of thinking. The prescriptions are familiar. Hire the right people. Set high goals. Confront the brutal facts. Fix the systems. Reengineer processes. Enhance quality. Streamline procedures. Instill a culture of discipline. Re-form and flatten the structure. Enhance interpersonal mechanics. Build skill inventories. Ideally the organization is like putty in the leader's hands.

This type of thinking sheds no light on why some organizations flourish despite the severest difficulties, whereas others, after being widely admired, suddenly collapse with the abruptness of a punctured balloon.

An alternative conception of leadership is that it swims in the richness and complexity of living. It breeds out of the connections between individuals. As an organizational participant, the leader grasps the interrelatedness of the people of the organization. The leader sees employees, clients, and partners as living, thinking, feeling individuals. Each individual has a history. Each individual is significant.

Storytelling embodies an approach that is well adapted to meet these deeper challenges of leadership. Whether a leader is persuading the organization to adopt an unfamiliar new idea or charting a future course for the organization or attracting the best talent or instilling passion and discipline throughout the organization or getting individuals to work together or getting them to continue believing in the leader through the unpredictable ups and downs of organizational life, storytelling can help—provided that the leader chooses the right kind of story for the task.

The underlying reason for the affinity between leadership and storytelling is simple: narrative—unlike abstractions and analysis—is inherently collaborative. Storytelling helps leaders work with other individuals as coparticipants, not merely as objects or underlings. Storytelling helps strengthen leaders' connectedness with the world. Isn't this what all leaders need—a connectedness with the people they are seeking to lead?

Seven High-Value Forms of
Organizational Storytelling

If Your Objective Is . . .	You Need a Story That . . .	Your Story Will Need to . . .
1. To communicate a complex idea and spark action	• Is true • Has a single protagonist who is typical of your audience • Focuses on the positive outcome	• Be told with minimal detail
2. To communicate who you are	• Reveals some strength or vulnerability from your past • Is true • Is moving	• Be told with context
3. To transmit values	• Describes how the leadership dealt with adversity • Is relevant to the here and now • Is believed	• Be consistent with the actions of the leadership
4. To get people working together in a group or community	• Is moving • Is interesting to the listeners • Is a story about a subject on which the listeners also have stories	• Be told with the context • Create a shared basis for action
5. To tame the grapevine or neutralize negative gossip	• Reveals humor or incongruity either in the bad news or in the author of the bad news or in the storyteller • Is true	• Be a blend of truth and caring for the object of the humor

You Will Also Need to . . .	Your Story Will Use or Inspire Such Phrases as . . .	When Your Story Is Successful . . .
• Frame the story so that the audience is listening • Provide guiderails that direct the listener toward the hoped-for insight	• "Just think . . ." • "Just imagine . . ." • "What if . . .	Your audience will grasp the idea and be stimulated to launch into action.
• Make sure the audience has the time and the interest to hear your story	• "I didn't know that about you!" • "How interesting!"	Your audience will have a better understanding of who you are as a person and may begin to trust you.
• Make sure your actions are consistent with your story • Make sure the context of your story fits the listeners	• "That's so right!" • "We should do that all the time!"	Your audience will understand how things are done around here.
• Establish an open agenda • Engender a process of story swapping • Have an action plan ready	• "That reminds me: I've got a story like that . . ." • "I like to hear more about that."	Your audience will be more ready to work together as a team, a group, or a community.
• Make sure that the bad news is indeed untrue or unreasonable • Commit yourself to telling the truth, however difficult that may be	• "You've got to be kidding!" • "I'd never thought about it like that before!"	Your audience will realize that the gossip or the bad news is either untrue or unreasonable.

(continued)

151

Seven High-Value Forms of
Organizational Storytelling *(continued)*

If Your Objective Is . . .	You Need a Story That . . .	Your Story Will Need to . . .
6. To share information and knowledge	• Includes the problem, the setting, the solution, and the explanation • Captures the granularity of the relevant area of knowledge	• Reflect multiple perspectives and disciplines • Be focused on the difficulties and how they were dealt with • Allow for serendipity
7. To lead people into the future	• Is about the future • Is evocative • Captures the basic idea of where you are heading • Focuses on a positive outcome	• Be told with as little detail as needed for understanding the idea • Resonate with the listeners

You Will Also Need to . . .	Your Story Will Use or Inspire Such Phrases as . . .	When Your Story Is Successful . . .
• Verify that the story is in fact true • Cross-check with other experiences • Keep a lookout for a better explanation	• "We'd better watch that in future!"	Your audience will understand how to do something and why.
• Provide additional context from the past and the present • Make sure that people are ready to follow (if not, use a type 1 story, that is, a story to spark action)	• "When do we start?" • "Let's do it!"	Your audience will understand where they are heading.

NOTES

Preface

Epigraph: J. Bruner, *Making Stories: Law, Literature, Life* (New York: Farrar, Straus & Giroux, 2002), p. 89.

1. Among the leadership books that touch on storytelling are W. Bennis, *On Becoming a Leader: The Leadership Classic Updated and Expanded* (Cambridge, Mass.: Perseus, 2003); H. Gardner, *Leading Minds: An Anatomy of Leadership* (New York: Basic Books, 1996); J. M. Kouzes and B. Z. Posner, *The Leadership Challenge* (San Francisco: Jossey-Bass, 2002); N. M. Tichy, *The Leadership Engine: Building Leaders at Every Level* (New York: HarperBusiness, 1997).

2. B. Birchard, "Once Upon a Time," *strategy+business*, Second Quarter 2002. [http://www.strategy-business.com/press/article/18637?pg=0].

3. Aristotle, *Poetics* (Indianapolis: Hackett, 1987).

4. Ovid, *Metamorphoses* (New York: Oxford University Press, 1998); G. Boccaccio, *The Decameron* (New York: Signet, 2002); H. Haddawy (trans.), *The Arabian Nights* (New York: Knopf, 1992); M. Twain, *Mississippi Writings: Tom Sawyer, Life on the Mississippi, Huckleberry Finn, Pudd'nhead Wilson*

(New York: Library of America, 1982); J. Campbell, *The Hero with a Thousand Faces* (New York: Meridian Books, 1956); D. Decker, *Anatomy of a Screenplay* (Los Angeles: Screenwriters Group, 1998); R. McKee, *Story: Substance, Structure, Style and the Principles of Screenwriting* (New York: HarperCollins, 1997).

5. Writers who apply this kind of thinking to organizational storytelling include Yannis Gabriel and Annette Simmons: see Y. Gabriel, *Storytelling in Organizations: Facts, Fictions, and Fantasies* (New York: Oxford University Press, 2001); A. Simmons, *The Story Factor* (Cambridge, Mass.: Perseus, 2000).

6. In this book *narrative* and *story* are used as synonyms, with a broad meaning that includes an account or anything narrated. Traditionalists might question whether some examples are "genuine" stories or merely ideas for possible stories yet to be told. In practice the usage of the word *story* is very broad. Donald Polkinghorne and others have suggested that we accept this broad usage: see D. E. Polkinghorne, *Narrative Knowing and the Human Sciences* (Albany, N.Y.: State University of New York Press, 1988). Within the broad field of *story*, we can then distinguish classically structured stories, well-made stories, anti-stories, fragmentary stories, stories with no ending, stories with multiple endings, stories with multiple beginnings, stories with endings that circle back to the beginning, comedies, tragedies, detective stories, romances, folk tales, novels, plays, movies, television miniseries, and so on, without the need to get into philosophical discussions as to what is "truly" a story. In common usage *story* is a large tent, with many variations under that tent. Some variations are more useful for some purposes than others. There are probably many variations that haven't yet been identified. If we start out with predetermined ideas of what a "real" story is, we

may end up missing useful forms of narratives. For an example of this phenomenon, see Gabriel, *Storytelling in Organizations*.

7. Aesop, *Aesop's Fables* (New York: SeaStar Books, 2000); J. de La Fontaine, *Fables* (New York: Everyman, 2001); F. Kafka, *The Metamorphosis* (New York: Bantam Books, 1972); G. Orwell, *Animal Farm* (New York: Signet, 1996); J. Agee, "A Mother's Tale," in R. Hansen and J. Shepard (eds.), *You've Got to Read This* (New York: HarperCollins, Perennial, 2000); D. Quinn, *Ishmael: An Adventure of the Mind and Spirit* (New York: Bantam Books, 1995); S. Johnson, *Who Moved My Cheese? An Amazing Way to Deal with Change in Your Work and in Your Life* (New York: Putnam, 1998).

8. In researching for this book, I discovered that the figure is 50 percent: see L. H. Lapham, M. Pollan, and E. Etheridge (eds.), *The Harper's Index Book* (New York: Henry Holt, 1984), p. 55.

9. A kinder, gentler inspiration also came from Grace Marmor Spruch's book *Squirrels at My Window: Life with a Remarkable Gang of Urban Squirrels* (Boulder, Colo.: Johnson Books, 2000), in which a scientist meticulously describes the life and times of a group of real-life city squirrels, whose personalities and foibles are not too removed from those of humans.

10. There are myriad real-life examples of companies in decline. These organizations are not in trouble because their managers are involved in systematic illegality, malfeasance, or fraud. They are not run by crooks. In fact their managers are generally intelligent and committed. They have shown leadership ability in the past. They are working long hours and trying very hard. They have not been blindsided by something that could not have been predicted. Often these firms even have fine reputations—they include some of the most

famous companies in the world. To cite just a few: General
Motors in the period from 1970 to 1990; IBM from 1988 to
1993; Motorola in its handling of digital technology for
mobile phones from 1990 to 1997; Rubbermaid from 1993 to
1998; A&P from 1960 to 1990; Firestone Tire & Rubber in
its handling of radial tires in the 1970s. For a discussion of the
issues, see J. Collins, *Good to Great: Why Some Companies
Make the Leap—And Others Don't* (New York: Harper-
Collins, 2001); S. Finkelstein, *Why Smart Executives Fail:
What You Can Learn from Their Mistakes* (New York: Portfolio, 2003); D. Sull, "Why Good Companies Go Bad," *Harvard Business Review,* July–Aug. 1999, pp. 42–48.

Part One

Epigraph: H. Miller, *Tropic of Capricorn* (New York: Grove Press,
1987), p. 35.

Chapter One

Epigraph: L. H. Lapham, M. Pollan, and E. Etheridge (eds.), *The
Harper's Index Book* (New York: Henry Holt, 1984), p. 55.

1. This thought has been attributed to E. M. Forster.
2. Diana is the Latin name of the Greek goddess Artemis, who
   was Apollo's twin sister and a daughter of Zeus. The goddess
   of chastity, Diana was a virgin huntress. In paintings and
   sculptures she was shown carrying a bow and a quiver of
   arrows. By some quirk she also presided over childbirth and
   was associated with the moon. See, for example, J. Weigel,
   Mythology for the Modern Reader (Lincoln, Neb.: Centennial
   Press, 1974).
3. The conventional wisdom that the way to get people to
   change is by giving them a reason is reflected in J. Kotter,
   Leading Change (Boston: Harvard Business School Press,
   1996). Kotter's more recent book, *The Heart of Change: Real-*

Life Stories of How People Change Their Organizations (Boston: Harvard Business School Press, 2002), continues the theme. The main difference between the two books is that in the latter, Kotter recommends giving people better reasons, an approach that is no more likely to succeed than his earlier recommendation. Other writers propose structural solutions, such as creating an autonomous organization to pursue the innovation as an opportunity rather than as a threat (C. M. Christensen and M. E. Raynor, *The Innovator's Solution: Creating and Sustaining Successful Growth* [Boston: Harvard Business School Press, 2003], pp. 113, 191) or financing an innovation marketplace (G. Hamel and L. Valikangas, "The Quest for Resilience," *Harvard Business Review*, Sept. 2003, p. 52). Structural approaches to creating innovation defer the problem, rather than solve it. Even if such measures are adopted, they do not obviate the need at some point to persuade the parent organization to adopt the innovation.

Chapter One Sidebars

a. The happiness of a story's ending relates to the narrative that is told and not necessarily to all the events. As Richard Kearney points out, "Happy endings often included . . . some rather punitive experiences for the evil characters—for example Snow White's stepmother is forced to dance herself to death in red-hot shoes and Cinderella's sisters have their eyes pierced by doves" (*On Stories* [London: Routledge, 2002], p. 160).

Chapter Two

Epigraph: W. Gibson, "Broad Band Blues," June 21, 2001. Economist.com [http://www.alananthony.com/images2/Articles/Broadband_Blues.PDF], retrieved Jan. 25, 2004.

1. F.-N. Thomas and M. Turner, *Clear and Simple as the Truth: Writing Classic Prose* (Princeton, N.J.: Princeton University Press, 1994), p. 100.
2. Thomas and Turner, *Clear and Simple as the Truth*, p. 61.

Part Two

Epigraph: M. Turner, *The Literary Mind* (New York: Oxford University Press, 1996), p. 4.

Chapter Three

Epigraph: M. C. Bateson, *Composing a Life* (New York: Penguin Books, 1990), p. 34.

Chapter Four

Epigraph: D. McAdams, *The Stories We Live By: Personal Myths and the Making of the Self* (New York: Morrow, 1993). Similarly, Jerome Bruner notes that "the self is probably the most impressive work of art we ever produce, surely the most intricate" (*Making Stories: Law, Literature, Life* [New York: Farrar, Straus & Giroux, 2002], p. 14).

1. See the work of Paul Costello and the Center for Narrative Studies at [www.storywise.com], Dec. 4, 2003.
2. H. Gardner, *Leading Minds: An Anatomy of Leadership* (New York: Basic Books, 1996), pp. 43–44.
3. D. McAdams, *The Stories We Live By: Personal Myths and the Making of the Self* (New York: Morrow, 1993).
4. N. M. Tichy, *The Leadership Engine: Building Leaders at Every Level* (New York: HarperBusiness, 1997).
5. Some would argue that of all the elements constituting a brand—the logo, the images, the products and services, the places and the people of the organization—the most important element is the narrative that ties these other elements together: see M. Mark and C. S. Pearson, *The Hero and the*

Outlaw: Building Extraordinary Brands Through the Power of Archetypes (New York: McGraw-Hill, 2002); L. Vincent, *Legendary Brands: Unleashing the Power of Storytelling to Create a Winning Marketing Strategy* (Chicago: Dearborn, 2002).

Chapter Four Sidebars

a. Aristotle, *Poetics* (Indianapolis: Hackett, 1987).
b. R. McKee, *Story: Substance, Structure, Style and the Principles of Screenwriting* (New York: HarperCollins, 1997), p. 181.
C. M. Mark and C. S. Pearson, *The Hero and the Outlaw: Building Extraordinary Brands Through the Power of Archetypes* (New York: McGraw-Hill, 2002); L. Vincent, *Legendary Brands: Unleashing the Power of Storytelling to Create a Winning Marketing Strategy* (Chicago: Dearborn, 2002); G. Zaltman, *How Customers Think: Essential Insights into the Mind of the Market* (Boston: Harvard Business School Press, 2003).

Chapter Five

Epigraph: M. Hammer and J. Champy, *Reengineering the Corporation: A Manifesto for Business Revolution* (New York: HarperBusiness, 1993), pp. 18–30. Hammer and Champy are correct in their diagnosis: we do need something entirely different. Their prognosis however is flawed. Their book recommends essentially "more of the same." Whether it's called *engineering* or *reengineering*, it's the same approach that mistakenly looks on an organization merely as a machine.

1. A good description of the personal interactions in a firm in a spiral of decline can be found in R. M. Kanter, "Leadership and the Psychology of Turnarounds," *Harvard Business Review,* June 2003, p. 58.
2. For an interesting description of a community and its importance, see A. MacIntyre, "A Partial Response to My Critics,"

161

in J. Horton and S. Mendus (eds.), *After MacIntyre: Critical Perspectives on the Work of Alasdair MacIntyre* (Notre Dame, Ind.: University of Notre Dame Press, 1994), p. 283.

3. J. B. Ciulla, *The Working Life: The Promise and Betrayal of Modern Work* (New York: Three Rivers Press, 2001), p. 150; see also D. Snowden, "Story Circles and Heuristic Based Interventions," *Knowledge Management*, July 2000, 3(10), 15–19.

4. Bringing people together physically is ideal. Is it possible to bring people together virtually, given the need for faster action and lower costs? Clearly where employees are scattered around the world and resources are not available to bring them together physically, a virtual get-together is better than not meeting at all. The communities of practice at Buckman Laboratories are an example of virtual gatherings that have proven effective.

5. All organizations eventually discover that knowledge sharing happens systematically only in informal networks or communities of practice. Moreover, it's often just as important to have knowledge shared between different fields of expertise. However, each branch of knowledge has its own set of terminology and rituals and experts. So when individuals are brought together from different fields, they tend to find difficulty in communicating with each other. See J. S. Brown, S. Denning, K. Groh, and L. Prusak, *The Narrative Lens* (Boston: Elsevier, forthcoming); E. Wenger, R. McDermott, and W. M. Snyder, *Cultivating Communities of Practice* (Boston: Harvard Business School Press, 2002).

6. One of the principal reasons for the failure of mergers and acquisitions is the clash of cultures. Often top management is bringing together individuals who have been fighting each other as competitors, maybe for generations. They are then expected to work together as if they were old friends. The

reality is that this won't happen until the individuals understand each other better, through hearing each other's stories and seeing the stories' meaning. If nothing is done, stories will be shared anyway—perhaps toxically—over a period of years. But when the process of constructive storytelling can be accelerated, then the two groups can merge productively and rapidly. On the multiple failures of mergers and acquisitions, see M. L. Sirower, *The Synergy Trap: How Companies Lose the Acquisition Game* (New York: Free Press, 1997).

7. Leading companies are moving toward federated planning in supply chain management. Supply chain partners collaborate to address trade-offs and break constraints across the extended enterprise. The traditional way of looking at a supply chain is to conceive of the organization being supplied as the commander of all the organizations providing products or services. As a result communications tend to flow in a single direction. The suggestions of the suppliers are not put on the table. What the best firms do is to treat their suppliers as genuine partners. This can seem strange at first, because the suppliers are used to being treated as subordinates. Fostering a federation with suppliers can help those suppliers to see themselves as genuine partners. See, for example, T. Laseter and K. Oliver, "When Will Supply Chain Management Grow Up?" in strategy+business, Fall 2003. [http://www. strategy-business.com/press/article/03304?pg=0].

Chapter Six

Epigraph: D. Berlinski, *A Tour of the Calculus* (New York: Vintage, 1997).

1. See, for example, C. Hymowitz, "CEOs Work Hard to Maintain the Faith in the Corner Office," *Wall Street Journal*, July 9, 2002; C. Hymowitz, "Do You Tell Your Staff When You Disagree with the Boss's Orders?" *Wall Street Journal*, Apr. 16, 2002.

2. Hymowitz, "Do You Tell Your Staff . . ."
3. The great religious teachers used parables to transmit values.
   The Greek word for *parable* implies two things laid side by
   side for comparison. Parables in the Christian tradition fea-
   ture ordinary events. A farmer sows his seed. A rich man
   accuses his manager of wasting his possessions. A man works
   in a vineyard. There is usually a surprise in these "ordinary"
   stories—an unexpected twist of the plot. How could a master
   praise his dishonest manager? How could a member of an
   underclass be the hero of a story? What landlord would let
   tenant farmers kill one servant after another, then send his
   son to be murdered too? Religious parables are similar to
   springboard stories, except that unlike a springboard story,
   they usually make no explicit claim that the event described
   actually happened. See, for example, the biblical parable of
   the talents (Matthew 25:14).

Chapter Seven

Epigraph: W. Shakespeare, *Hamlet* (II, ii, 203–204).
1. For the dangers of adopting a stance of habitual irony, see A.
   MacIntyre, *Dependent Rational Animals: Why Human
   Beings Need the Virtues* (Chicago: Open Court, 1999) pp.
   151–154.
2. M. Bakhtin, *Rabelais and His World* (Bloomington: Indiana
   University Press, 1984), p. 11.

Chapter Eight

Epigraph: D. Deutsch, *The Fabric of Reality: The Science of Parallel Universes—And Its Implications* (New York: Allen Lane,
   1997), p. 30.
1. A story told by British philosopher Bertrand Russell; discussed
   in Deutsch, *The Fabric of Reality*, pp. 60–61.
2. Werner Heisenberg pointed out that what we observe is not

nature itself but nature exposed to our method of questioning ("Quantum Mechanics, 1925–1927: Implications of Uncertainty" [www.aip.org/history/heisenberg/p08c.htm], Nov. 24, 2003). If one limits one's observations to a single field of expertise, one is seeing the world through the lens of that particular field of expertise. To get a more rounded perspective, one should observe the same phenomenon from the perspectives of other disciplines.

3. Deutsch, *The Fabric of Reality*, p. 30.
4. See D. Snowden, "Story Circles and Heuristic Based Interventions," *Knowledge Management*, July 2000, 3(10), 15–19; D. Snowden, "Complex Acts of Knowing—Paradox and Descriptive Self-Awareness," *Journal of Knowledge Management*, May 2002, 6(2), 100–111.

Chapter Nine

Epigraph: T. Bulfinch, *Mythology* (New York: Dell, 1959), p. 185.
1. J. Magretta, "Why Business Models Matter," *Harvard Business Review*, May 2002, p. 86.
2. Preparing for every eventuality is impossible for most organizations. For one thing it's too expensive. So organizations make trade-offs between risks and returns. In choosing which risks to prepare for, the plausibility of each scenario becomes an issue.
3. Brazilian proverb.
4. N. M. Tichy, *The Leadership Engine: Building Leaders at Every Level* (New York: HarperBusiness, 1997).
5. "In the sharp formulation of the law of causality—'if we know the present exactly, we can calculate the future'—it is not the conclusion that is wrong but the premise" (Heisenberg, in uncertainty principle paper, 1927): see "Quantum Mechanics, 1925–1927: Implications of Uncertainty" [www.aip.org/history/heisenberg/p08c.htm], Nov. 24, 2003.

6. For more on springboard stories, see Chapters One and Two; also see S. Denning, *The Springboard: How Storytelling Ignites Action in Knowledge-Era Organizations* (Boston: Butterworth Heinemann, 2000).

Chapter Ten

Epigraph: J. Bruner, *Making Stories: Law, Literature, Life* (New York: Farrar, Straus & Giroux, 2002), p. 94.

1. Working backward from a preferred future can sometimes be more effective than working forward: see E. Lindaman, *Thinking in Future Tense* (Nashville, Tenn.: Broadman Press, 1978); M. Connolly and R. Rianoshek, *The Communication Catalyst* (Chicago: Dearborn, 2002), pp. 124–125.

2. Consider, for example, the inaction of Motorola in the face of the emergence of digital phones, the inability of Rubbermaid to become more efficient in the period from 1993 to 1997, the complacency of Digital Equipment Corporation in the face of the emergence of PCs, and the failure of Firestone Tire & Rubber to respond to the challenge of radial tires: see S. Finkelstein, *Why Smart Executives Fail: What You Can Learn from Their Mistakes* (New York: Portfolio, 2003); D. Sull, "Why Good Companies Go Bad," *Harvard Business Review*, July–Aug. 1999, pp. 42-48; J. Collins, *Good to Great: Why Some Companies Make the Leap—And Others Don't* (New York: HarperCollins, 2001).

3. For example, Quaker Oats's purchase of Snapple in 1994 and GM's $45 billion venture into robotics in the 1980s: see Finkelstein, *Why Smart Executives Fail*.

4. For example, the launch of SAP by former employees of IBM.

5. See R. M. Kanter, "Leadership and the Psychology of Turnarounds," *Harvard Business Review*, June 2003, pp. 58–67.

Part Three

Epigraph: A. MacIntyre, *After Virtue* (2nd ed.), (Notre Dame, Ind.: University of Notre Dame Press, 1984), p. 216.

Chapter Eleven

Epigraph: R. A. Heifetz and M. Linsky, *Leadership on the Line: Staying Alive Through the Dangers of Leading.* (Boston: Harvard Business School Press, 2002), pp. 13–14.

1. F.-N. Thomas and M. Turner, *Clear and Simple as the Truth: Writing Classic Prose* (Princeton, N.J.: Princeton University Press, 1994), p. 34.

2. M. K. de Vries, *The Leadership Mystique: A User's Manual for the Human Enterprise* (Upper Saddle River, N.J.: Prentice Hall, 2001).

3. See "Pericles' Funeral Oration," in Thucydides, *History of the Peloponnesian War* (Book II), (New York: Penguin Books, 1954).

Chapter Twelve

Epigraph: J. Bruner, *Making Stories: Law, Literature, Life* (New York: Farrar, Straus & Giroux, 2002), p. 93.

Further Reading

Storytelling to Communicate
Complex Ideas and Spark Action
(Chapters One and Two)

On stories that spark change and introduce new ideas:

Davenport, T., and Prusak, L. *What's the Big Idea?* Boston: Harvard Business School Press, 2003.

Denning, S. *The Springboard: How Storytelling Ignites Action in Knowledge-Era Organizations.* Boston: Butterworth Heinemann, 2000.

On parable and metaphor:

Lakoff, G., and Johnson, M. *The Metaphors We Live By.* Chicago: University of Chicago Press, 1983.

Turner, M. *The Literary Mind.* New York: Oxford University Press, 1996.

Storytelling to Reveal Who You Are
(Chapter Four)

On the source of identity in narrative:

Bruner, J. *Making Stories: Law, Literature, Life.* New York: Farrar, Straus & Giroux, 2002.

Eakin, P. J. *How Our Lives Become Stories: Making Selves.* Ithaca, N.Y.: Cornell University Press, 2001.

Linde, C. *Life Stories: The Creation of Coherence.* New York: Oxford University Press, 1993.

McAdams, D. P. *The Stories We Live By: Personal Myths and the Making of the Self.* New York: Morrow, 1993.

On the use of identity stories for leaders:

Bennis, W. *On Becoming a Leader: The Leadership Classic Updated and Expanded.* Cambridge, Mass.: Perseus, 2003.

Gardner, H. *Leading Minds: An Anatomy of Leadership.* New York: Basic Books, 1996.

Tichy, N. M. *The Leadership Engine: Building Leaders at Every Level.* New York: HarperBusiness, 1997.

On the role of stories in brands and marketing:

Mark, M., and Pearson, C. S. *The Hero and the Outlaw: Building Extraordinary Brands Through the Power of Archetypes.* New York: McGraw-Hill, 2002.

Vincent, L. *Legendary Brands: Unleashing the Power of Storytelling to Create a Winning Marketing Strategy.* Chicago: Dearborn, 2002.

Zaltman, G. *How Customers Think: Essential Insights into the Mind of the Market.* Boston: Harvard Business School Press, 2003.

Storytelling to Get Individuals to Work Together (Chapter Five)

Horton, J., and Mendus, S. (eds.). *After MacIntyre: Critical Perspectives on the Work of Alasdair MacIntyre.* Notre Dame, Ind.: University of Notre Dame Press, 1994.

Kahan, S. "Jumpstart Storytelling." [www.sethkahan.com], Nov. 9, 2003.

MacIntyre, A. *Dependent Rational Animals: Why Human Beings Need the Virtues*. Chicago: Open Court, 1999.

Prusak, L., and Cohen, D. *In Good Company*. Boston: Harvard Business School Press, 2001.

Wenger, E., McDermott, R., and Snyder, W. M. *Cultivating Communities of Practice*. Boston: Harvard Business School Press, 2002.

Storytelling to Transmit Values
(Chapter Six)

On the role of storytelling in establishing values:

Horton, J., and Mendus, S. (eds.). *After MacIntyre: Critical Perspectives on the Work of Alasdair MacIntyre*. Notre Dame, Ind.: University of Notre Dame Press, 1994.

MacIntyre, A. *After Virtue*. (2nd ed.) Notre Dame, Ind.: University of Notre Dame, 1984.

Storytelling to Tame the Grapevine
(Chapter Seven)

On the subject of humor:

Bakhtin, M. *Rabelais and His World*. Bloomington: Indiana University Press, 1984.

Cohen, T. *Jokes: Philosophical Thoughts on Joking Matters*. Chicago: University of Chicago Press, 2001.

On satire and satirical metaphors:

Egan, G. *Working the Shadow Side: A Guide to Positive Behind-the-Scenes Management*. San Francisco: Jossey-Bass, 1994.

Hill, W. F., and Ottchen, C. J. *Shakespeare's Insults: Educating Your Wit*. Cambridge, England: Mainsail Press, 1991.

Hodgart, M. *Satire*. London: World University Library, 1969.

Leach, M. *The Ultimate Insult.* London: Michael O'Mara Books, 1996.

Lyneham, P. *Political Speak: The Bemused Voter's Guide to Insults, Promises, Leadership Coups, Media Grabs, Pork-Barreling and Old Fashioned Double-Speak.* Sydney: ABC Books, 1991.

Odean, K. *High Steppers, Fallen Angels and Lollipops: Wall Street Slang.* New York: Henry Holt, 1989.

Rosner, J. *The Hater's Handbook.* New York: Dell, 1965.

Smith, D. S. *Down-Home Talk: An Outrageous Dictionary of Colorful Country Expressions.* London: Collier Books, 1988.

Storytelling to Share Knowledge (Chapter Eight)

On the role of story in decision making:

Klein, G. *Sources of Power: How People Make Decisions.* Cambridge, Mass.: MIT, 1999.

Orr, J. *Talking About Machines: An Ethnography of a Modern Job.* Ithaca, N.Y.: Cornell University Press, 1996.

On knowledge as explanation:

Deutsch, D. *The Fabric of Reality: The Science of Parallel Universes—And Its Implications.* New York: Allen Lane, 1997.

Lawson, H. *Closure: The Story of Everything.* London: Routledge, 2001.

On knowledge management:

Amidon, D. *Innovation Strategy for the Knowledge Economy: The Ken Awakening.* Boston: Butterworth Heinemann, 1997.

Brown, J. S., and Duguid, P. *The Social Life of Information.* Boston: Harvard Business School Press, 2000.

Collison, C., and Parcell, G. *Learning to Fly.* London: Capstone, 2001.

Cross, R., and Prusak, L. "The People Who Make Organizations Go—Or Stop." *Harvard Business Review*, June 2002, p. 104.

Davenport, T., and Prusak, L. *Working Knowledge.* Boston: Harvard Business School Press, 1998.

Denning, S. *The Springboard: How Storytelling Ignites Action in Knowledge-Era Organizations.* Boston: Butterworth Heinemann, 2000.

Kurtz, C., and Snowden, D. "The New Dynamics of Strategy: Sense Making in a Complex-Complicated World." *IBM Systems Journal*, 2003, 42(3), 462–483.

Rumizen, M. *The Complete Idiot's Guide to Knowledge Management.* Indianapolis: Alpha, 2002.

Snowden, D. "Complex Acts of Knowing—Paradox and Descriptive Self-Awareness." *Journal of Knowledge Management*, May 2002, 6(2), 100–111.

Snowden, D. "Narrative Patterns: The Perils and Possibilities of Using Story in Organisations." In E. Lesser and L. Prusak (eds.), *Value-Added Knowledge: Insights from the IBM Institute for Knowledge-Based Organizations.* New York: Oxford University Press, 2003.

Storytelling to Create a Future (Chapter Nine)

On business models and scenarios:

de Geus, A. *The Living Company: Habits for Survival in a Turbulent Business Environment.* Boston: Harvard Business School Press, 1997.

Magretta, J. "Why Business Models Matter." *Harvard Business Review*, May 2002, pp. 86–92.

Schwartz, P. *The Art of the Long View: Planning for the Future in an Uncertain World.* New York: Doubleday, 1996.

Van Der Heijden, K. *Scenarios: The Art of Strategic Conversation.* New York: Wiley, 1996.

On communicating a vision:

Carse, J. P. *Finite and Infinite Games.* New York: Ballantine, 1994.

Lindaman, E. *Thinking in Future Tense.* Nashville, Tenn.: Broadman Press, 1978.

Quinn, D. *Beyond Civilization: Humanity's Next Great Adventure.* New York: Harmony Books, 1999.

On appreciative inquiry:

Srivastva, S., Cooperrider, D. L., and Associates. *Appreciative Management and Leadership: The Power of Positive Thought and Action in Organizations.* San Francisco: Jossey-Bass, 1990.

Whitney, D., and Trosten-Bloom, A. *The Power of Appreciative Inquiry: A Practical Guide to Positive Change.* San Francisco: Berrett-Koehler, 2003.

Role of Stories Generally

On the nature of story:

Aristotle. *Poetics.* Indianapolis: Hackett, 1987.

Aristotle. *The Art of Rhetoric.* New York: Penguin Books, 1991.

Boje, D. *Narrative Methods for Organizational and Communication Research.* Thousand Oaks, Calif.: Sage, 2001.

Campbell, J. *The Hero with a Thousand Faces.* New York: Meridian Books, 1956.

Decker, D. *Anatomy of a Screenplay.* Los Angeles: Screenwriters Group, 1998.

Fulford, R. *The Triumph of Narrative: Storytelling in the Age of Mass Culture.* Toronto: Anansi Press: 1999.

Kearney, R. *On Stories.* London: Routledge, 2001.

Kearney, R. *Strangers, Gods and Monsters.* London: Routledge, 2003.

McKee, R. *Story: Substance, Structure, Style and the Principles of Screenwriting*. New York: HarperCollins, 1997.

On the relationship between narrative and paradigmatic thinking:

Bruner, J. *Actual Minds, Possible Worlds*. Cambridge, Mass.: Harvard University Press, 1986.

Bruner, J. *Acts of Meaning*. Cambridge, Mass.: Harvard University Press, 1990.

Bruner, J. *Making Stories: Law, Literature, Life*. New York: Farrar, Straus & Giroux, 2002.

Nash, C. *Narrative in Culture: The Uses of Storytelling in the Sciences, Philosophy and Literature*. London: Routledge, 1990.

Polkinghorne, D. E. *Narrative Knowing and the Human Sciences*. Albany, N.Y.: State University of New York Press, 1988.

On storytelling in organizations:

Davenport, T., and Prusak, L. *What's the Big Idea?* Boston: Harvard Business School Press, 2003.

Denning, S. *The Springboard: How Storytelling Ignites Action in Knowledge-Era Organizations*. Boston: Butterworth Heinemann, 2000.

Gabriel, Y. *Storytelling in Organizations: Facts, Fictions, and Fantasies*. New York: Oxford University Press, 2001.

Neuhauser, P. *Corporate Legends and Lore: The Power of Storytelling as a Management Tool*. New York: McGraw-Hill, 1993.

Simmons, A. *The Story Factor*. Cambridge, Mass.: Perseus, 2000.

Performing the story:

Lipman, D. *Improving Your Storytelling: Beyond the Basics for All Who Tell Stories in Work or Play*. Little Rock, Ark.: August House, 1999.

Stanislavski, K. *An Actor Prepares*. New York: Theatre Arts Books, 1989.

The Nature of Leadership

Bennis, W. *On Becoming a Leader: The Leadership Classic Updated and Expanded.* Cambridge, Mass.: Perseus, 2003.

Bolman, L., and Deal, T. *Leading with Soul: An Uncommon Journey of Spirit.* (Rev. ed.) San Francisco: Jossey-Bass, 2001.

Collins, J. *Good to Great: Why Some Companies Make the Leap—And Others Don't.* New York: HarperCollins, 2001.

Finkelstein, S. *Why Smart Executives Fail: What You Can Learn from Their Mistakes.* New York: Portfolio, 2003.

Gardner, H. *Leading Minds: An Anatomy of Leadership.* New York: Basic Books, 1996.

George, B. *Authentic Leadership: Rediscovering the Secrets to Creating Lasting Value.* San Francisco: Jossey-Bass, 2003.

Goleman, D. *Primal Leadership: Realizing the Power of Emotional Intelligence.* Boston: Harvard Business School Press, 2002.

Heifetz, R., and Linsky, M. *Leadership on the Line: Staying Alive Through the Dangers of Leading.* Boston: Harvard Business School Press, 2002.

Kouzes, J. M., and Posner, B. Z. *The Leadership Challenge.* San Francisco: Jossey-Bass, 2002.

Sull, D. "Why Good Companies Go Bad." *Harvard Business Review,* July–Aug. 1999, pp. 42–48.

Tichy, N. M. *The Leadership Engine: Building Leaders at Every Level.* New York: HarperBusiness, 1997.

Write to the Author

In this book I have shared what I have learned from many sources. There is much more to learn. I invite readers to participate with me in an ongoing dialogue to deepen everyone's understanding of leadership and storytelling.

I would welcome hearing your questions, your successes and setbacks, your hopes and fears. If anything in this book has touched you, troubled you, or opened new possibilities for you, I'd like to hear about it. Please write to me, and I'll do my best to respond to you and orchestrate an ongoing conversation. Through shared dialogue, I hope to keep finding new ways to breathe energy and delight into life and work.

You can contact me by e-mail or through my Web site:

E-mail: steve@stevedennning.com
Internet: www.stevedenning.com

I'm looking forward to hearing from you.

Acknowledgments

M any people have contributed to the creation of this book. I have received many helpful comments through my Web site, from those participating in the improv theater event that took place in Washington, D.C., in May 2003, and from the members of the Golden Fleece Group in Washington, D.C. At the risk of slighting some by mentioning others, I would particularly like to thank: Jerry Ash, Madelyn Blair, Ann Bracken, Susan Burton, Paul Costello, Sharon Cox, Rob Creekmore, Kelly Cresap, Karen Dietz, Lyn Dowling, Svend-Erik Engh, Lucia Edmonds, Lynne Feingold, Jane Flareup, Larry Forster, Harriet Gabbert, Joan Girardi, Donald Hawkins, Seth Kahan, Ruth Keeting-White, Alicia Korten, Lisa Kimball, Kent Lineback, Elspeth MacHattie, Joseph Mancini Jr., Michael Margolis, Anne Orban, Debi Orton, Larry Prusak, Ashraf Ramzy, John Sadowsky, Sandy Schuman, Lesley Shneier, Dave Snowden, Karen Solit, Richard Stone, Kathe Sweeney, Dirk Walvoord, and Juanita Weaver.

About the Author

Stephen (Steve) Denning was born and educated in Sydney, Australia. He studied law and psychology at Sydney University and worked as a lawyer in Sydney for several years. He then earned a postgraduate degree in law at Oxford University. In 1969, he joined the World Bank, where he held various management positions, including director of the Southern Africa Department, from 1990 to 1994, and director of the Africa Region, from 1994 to 1996. From 1996 to 2000, he was program director, Knowledge Management at the World Bank and spearheaded the organizational knowledge-sharing program.

Steve is the author of *The Springboard: How Storytelling Ignites Action in Knowledge-Era Organizations* (Butterworth Heinemann, 2000), which describes how storytelling can serve as a powerful tool for organizational change, including the introduction of knowledge management.

In November 2000, Steve was selected as one of the world's ten Most Admired Knowledge Leaders (Teleos). Since

2000, he has been working with organizations in the United States, Europe, Asia, and Australia on organizational storytelling and knowledge management. In April 2003, he was ranked among the world's Top Two Hundred Business Gurus by Thomas Davenport and Laurence Prusak in their book *What's the Big Idea?* From 1993 to 1996, he was a member of the Conference Board's Quality Council V. He is a Fellow of the Royal Society of Arts, and he has published a novel and a volume of poetry.

Steve's Web site, containing a collection of materials on organizational storytelling and knowledge management, may be found at www.stevedenning.com.